Also by Sean-Michael Green:

Marching to College

Advance Praise for
The Things I Learned in College

"This is an ambitious and excellent work, well written and laced with dry humor. Even the chapter subheadings are funny . . . Five stars to *The Things I Learned in College*."
- Publishers Daily Reviews

"Beyond the witty experiences, Green takes readers through the real ups and downs of the Ivy League, leaving them with a sense of the heartfelt relationships and meaningful experiences of college life. Anyone looking to attend college, whether or not he or she is applying to the Ivy League schools, should read this book closely to get a more realistic picture of university life: the parties, the relationships, the laughs, the tears, and the nights you find yourself without a way to get home at three o'clock in the morning."
- Chanticleer Book Reviews

"Sean-Michael Green takes you on a year-long quest through all eight prestigious schools. He uncovers the history, traditions, and quirks of each campus. Green takes you on a fun-filled exploration of student life through his stories. Buyer beware: It's a journey of discovery that leaves you wanting more."
- Stan Phelps
  Author of *Purple Goldfish, Green Goldfish, Golden Goldfish,* and *Blue Goldfish*

"Amusing, insightful snapshots of Ivy League variegations."
- Kirkus

"Green's recounting of his time at the Ivy League, is probably one of the honest and compelling pieces of writing I've read . . ."
- Jesse at Bookishjessp.com

"Rather than spewing facts, Green gives readers a remarkable sense of the intangibles involved in Ivy League life . . . Certain aspects of a college cannot be found out from Googling it, and Green does an impressive job of relaying such crucial details."
- Thomas Roades
  The Caviler Daily
  University of Virginia

"Sean-Michael Green recalls many shocking and intriguing events in a thoughtful and light-hearted way, treating Brown, Columbia, Cornell, Dartmouth, Harvard, University of Pennsylvania, Princeton and Yale like old friends."
- Erika Lee
  The Daily Trojan
  University of Southern California

". . . an engaging and entertaining reading experience that uncovers the enigma of the Ivy League . . ."
- Kyle Tatich
  Old Gold & Black
  Wake Forest University

"What is great is that, as he is not an undergrad himself, his position as an outsider enables his reader to empathise with him instantly, and we embark on the same journey with the same curiosity and excitement he must have felt going on it."

    -   América Aguilera

"I loved being able to see these little glimpses into these schools . . . The book made me want to tour the colleges myself."

    -   Ashley at thebookfetishblog.com

"If you want to go to an Ivy League school, you need to read this book. If you don't care about college at all but want to be entertained, read this book. If you already have degrees from all eight Ivies, well, then I guess you're qualified to write the rebuttal."

    -   Shaun Eli Breidbart

       Comedian

       The Ivy League of Comedy

the THINGS
I LEARNED
IN COLLEGE:

MY YEAR IN THE IVY LEAGUE

Sean-Michael Green

For Donna Green.
I think she would have been proud.

TheLeigh Publishing Company, LLC
New Haven, CT   Pittsburgh, PA
www.TheLeigh.com

ISBN: 978-0-692-60317-8

Library of Congress Control Number: 2016900713

First Printing: 2016
Printed in the United States of America

This work is narrative nonfiction. Creative license has been taken,
especially in an effort to protect the privacy of individuals and groups.

TABLE OF CONTENTS

Contents

INTRODUCTION

It was two weeks before winter final exams at Yale University. I had no tests to take and no papers to write, but I was still anxious.

Everything that should have been green was white. The grass was buried under a fresh snowfall; tree limbs bent under the weight. Ivy and snow covered walls gave the buildings lining the street an unusual, textured appearance.

Despite the powdery snow, the day was beautiful. The cold was not uncomfortable, and the sidewalks were clear of snow and slush. A brilliant blue sky silhouetted majestic stone buildings. The walkway teemed with young men and women lugging books and backpacks. Most wore hats and coats, some wore lighter jackets, and at least one wore shorts and flip-flops. Some of the pedestrians chatted with each other or waved to passing friends, but the mood of the community was serious, purposeful.

I walked through the stone arch of Phelps gate, swept onto Old Campus by the stream of foot traffic. I glanced across the campus at the Harkness Tower. The students around me seemed to be oblivious to the ornately designed gothic stone tower, but my eyes were always drawn to it. It was a symbol of wealth and power and all things phallic, and I couldn't help but to look.

I made a sharp right and headed across campus. I passed Durfee Hall – one of the oldest buildings on campus – and crossed Elm Street. I was on the lookout for BMW-wielding teens from parts of the country not accustomed to snowy roads. In the past two days, I had seen three car accidents (or, measured differently, about $17,000 worth of accidents) where students braked too late in the snow and rear-ended other cars.

I was so worried about cars that I nearly lost my life to a middle-aged man on a bicycle. The man looked like he wanted to flip me the finger as he sped off, but he could not free his hand from his mitten fast enough.

3

Within two minutes, I entered Harkness Hall and took the stairs to the second floor. I passed two young girls chatting in the hallway, leaving as I was arriving. I recognized one of the girls, Kelly, and I smiled at her. Her face lit up when she saw me, and she stopped to introduce me to her friend. Kelly and her friend were discussing plans for Friday night. Apparently, their entire sorority had been invited to attend a naked party. Some of the sisters were outraged; some were intrigued.

"Do people actually have sex at naked parties?" I wondered.

"Well, not *real* sex," Kelly responded, her nose crinkling in disgust. "Just oral sex."

"But most of the guys just want to watch girls go down on each other," her friend added helpfully.

Kelly asked me, "So where are you going now? Do you want to get lunch with us?"

"I'd like to, but I have to get to a class right now."

"Well, send me an e-mail and maybe we can get together this weekend," she said, starting to move off. "And if you want to check out that party, I can send you the details."

After they entered the staircase, I walked past room 203 and stopped outside to collect my thoughts. I gathered my courage, doubled back to the room, and walked inside.

The classroom struck me as both beautiful and typical. Light hardwood floors supported individual desks that seemed too clean and new to be a part of a college campus. Two walls were a gray stone; a third was dominated by clean, dark chalkboards; and the fourth was a row of thick windows offering views of the Sterling Memorial Library.

As I slipped into the room, I saw a familiar face. Tony looked up at me, smiled and gave me a quick hand gesture. Tony was the person who recommended the class to me.

4

Since meeting Tony, I learned that he was allegedly a member of one of Yale's oldest secret societies: Skull and Bones. I had often passed the tomb where members spend their Thursday and Sunday evenings, imagining what wonders or horrors were unfolding inside the depths of the foreboding building. I, of course, had no practical way of exploring the tomb myself. I was not a Bonesman, and the society was intensely secretive. In fact, Tony never so much as implied to me that he might be a member of any secret society. But other Yale students had a sense of the ebb and flow of people around campus, and several students whispered of Tony's assumed membership in Bones.

I returned a genuine smile to Tony as I took a seat at the back of the room in the fifth row.

The room never filled. The 40 seats were taken by only 16 students who seemed to prefer the middle of the room. A couple of outliers sat in the first and fourth rows, but I was the only person in the very back. I wished I had sat a row or two forward.

Behind a simple, wooden lectern at the front of the room stood a professor in his early thirties. He surveyed a few pages of his notes, looking a bit harried. I sat for only a couple of minutes when he glanced at his watch and said, "Why don't we get started?"

He began by recapping the discussion from the last class. The course was titled, "Meta-Ethics," and the professor was an academic authority on the subject. He was a new professor, but he exuded confidence mixed with humility, and the students seemed to warm to him. Only one student was sleeping – and he was doing a brilliant job of it, complete with drool – while most of his peers took notes about a discussion that was presumably already outlined in their notes from the last class.

The discussion turned softly Socratic as students began asking questions and the professor returned the queries to the class. The topic of the moment was love and the "rules" of being in love. Tony offered a comment that seemed remarkably astute, considering that he was taking the philosophy class to satisfy a university graduation requirement rather than to complete his Engineering major. A girl identified as Lisa took issue with Tony's point. She began by making a sound of disgust like she had just bitten into a piece of rotten fruit. Prompted by the professor, she started to articulate her argument, but she did it with a tone of condescension that unnerved me. The prof continued to facilitate the exchange between Lisa and Tony, while I watched and listened with interest, jotting down notes in my notebook.

"And what do you think?" I looked up to find the professor addressing me. As I debated how to respond, he prodded, "Well, for example, what do you love?"

I decided to just go for honesty. "College."

A few students snickered. "I hope you mean Yale," the professor said.

"Of course," I agreed. "But I'm also a big fan of Dartmouth. And Harvard. And Cornell. And certainly Princeton. Oh, and Brown is great too." I tried to force myself to stop talking, but I could not suppress blurting out, quickly and in an unnaturally high octave, "And Penn and Columbia."

The class laughed and the professor looked at me intently. "And you are, Mister...?" he asked.

I cringed a bit. "Green."

"Mr. Green?" He paused, and I could feel him taking note of my 34 years. I had never felt less like an undergraduate student, which was appropriate, since I had not been an undergrad in many years.

"Uh, Professor?" Tony started. "Sean-Michael is the guy that I told you about."

The skepticism in the professor's face flashed to confusion before settling in a knowing smile. "Yes, that's right." Turning to the class-at-large, he said, "We have a guest among us. Mr. Green is here temporarily to observe

6

life in the Ivy League. I understand that he has spent the past few months at some of our peer universities, and, after Yale, he will visit the remainder of the schools. Is that right, Mr. Green?"

"Yes, sir," I responded. "I'm about halfway through the research now."

"And what have you learned so far?"

I thought back on the many classes I visited, the dozens of parties I attended, and the hundreds of students I met. I carefully considered how to answer the question, bearing in mind that the class was only scheduled for another half an hour.

*

I am, according to people who know me well, a college freak. The people who *really* know me call me a college snob. They may be right.

Higher education is my passion. The best analogy I can find (without resorting to words such as "obsessive") is to compare my affection for universities to my family's feeling for football.

My father and brothers watch a lot of football. They record the games that they miss and some of the ones that they watch. My father is known to shout out, "Yes!" or "No!" or "Holy Cats!" at the television set during a game. Watching a live game is a special treat, and the men in my family are prepared to drive up to 13 hours, if necessary, to see a game live. They will sit in the rain and pay $8 for nachos to watch players so distant that they look like tiny, broad shouldered insects. They know which players play for which teams, and they track the movements of those players throughout the League. They monitor statistics – historical and ongoing. My brothers and father discuss football with each other, their friends, the people who fix their cars, their dentists, etc. They talk about which teams will win or lose, who will get the most money, and how

7

they would revise coaching strategies given a chance. My brother, Jason, has even gone so far as to have a rather large Steelers tattoo placed on his left calf.

That's how I feel about higher education.

I watch school Web sites for changes and updates. A strategic hiring of a faculty member has been known to make me scream out, "Eek!" or "Wow!" at my computer monitor. I read *The Chronicle of Higher Education, University Business News*, and *College Bound* magazine. One of my favorite games to play – and, at the risk of sounding immodest, a game that I could easily represent our country in the Olympic Games – is to spot school stickers on the back of cars. I can pick out a Cornell sticker from two-tenths of a mile, and I can tell the difference between a Princeton sticker and a Syracuse sticker from twice that distance. I discuss higher education with my friends, family, mechanics, and medical professionals, most of whom quickly remember that they left their stoves on/forgot to pick up a relative from the airport/must answer their silently vibrating cell phones, and excuse themselves. I know how many students my favorite universities admit each year, what the Provosts of each of those schools studied in graduate school, and how much money university presidents make each year. I do not have a tattoo decrying my infatuation, but my casual attire almost always includes a shirt announcing the name of a school. (As I type this, I'm wearing a green Dartmouth shirt – one of my favorites.)

And I watch football, too. College football.

It is difficult to explain exactly what I like about universities. I love the complexities of the business of running a university. Universities are often physically beautiful places, with interesting architecture and idyllic campuses. Perhaps the best reason that I have for loving schools is because I love students. It is no small feat to leave home to study in the environment of a university. Despite the support that students receive, it is sink or swim, and not everyone swims. The growth spurt that adolescents experience in their early teens is matched intellectually and socially during college. Students live and study among their peers, surrounded by pressures that force them to explore their boundaries and abilities. As a result, schools often produce students who are eternally bonded to their institutions. They sport their school colors with pride and often make financial gifts to their universities. What other business inspires such loyalty among its clients?

As much as I like higher education, my affections are qualified. I believe that not all schools are created equal. I know that all schools have weaknesses, and that most schools have substantial strengths. In the world of colleges, however, there are some dogs and some saints. Sometimes the differences are subtle and almost always they are subjective, but I appreciate certain schools more than others.

The schools of the Ivy League are my favorites. The term, "Ivy League," was created to describe a college football conference. The first use of "ivy" in describing schools was by the sportswriter, Stanley Woodward in 1933. It was originally a group of four schools, and one of the alleged stories to explain the birth of the term "Ivy League" is that it came from Roman numeral "IV." However the term was born, it has expanded well beyond football in the minds of the masses.

The Ivy League includes eight schools: Brown, Columbia, Cornell, Dartmouth, Harvard, Penn, Princeton, and Yale. The schools are unique and possess their own quirks and personalities, but they share some common ground. They are all located in the northeast United States, and they move through four distinct seasons each year – although some seasons last longer than others. They sometimes make collective decisions on issues. For example, the Ivies have agreed among themselves not to offer athletic scholarships to students. Representatives of

9

the Ivy League schools often travel in packs to admissions events because they are seeking the same, rare students.

The Ivies also share a common victimization. They are often the target of myths and misconceptions. "Ivy League" can be an unfriendly and derogatory stereotype. It implies excessive wealth, underdeveloped social skills, and arrogance. Many people believe that, to get into an Ivy, all you need is to finance a new building or to have deep family connections. Once at the school, students lock themselves away from dating, parties, and pop culture to become grade-obsessed recluses, complete with thick glasses and pocket protectors; or, in the alternative, they become party-obsessed monsters armed with fake IDs and moms' credit cards. Diversity is all but absent at Ivy League schools, and the atmosphere fosters a sense of elitism. I have heard many people volunteer those reasons for not attending Ivy League schools.

Nevertheless, I have often heard students and alumni of non-Ivies attempt to tap into the Ivy League's reputation.

I had a friend – an alumnus of Emory University – who said to me, "You know, they call Emory 'the Ivy of the South?'"

I smiled and nodded, and I did not mention that I have also heard Stanford called the "Ivy of the West," Northwestern called the "Ivy of the Midwest," Hamilton called "a Little Ivy," and Smith called a "Sister Ivy."

A former co-worker of mine who went to Dickinson College was fond of saying that Dickinson was just like an Ivy League school, only located in Pennsylvania.

I smiled and nodded and did not mention that the University of Pennsylvania was much more like an Ivy League school located in Pennsylvania.

At a gas station once, a cashier noticed my Columbia t-shirt and told me it was nice to see it because she went to an Ivy League school as well. When I asked which school she went to, she said, "Bucknell."

I probably smiled and nodded – it is too traumatic for me to think about.

For a college freak/snob, I have a strange and sordid educational history. I was an academically horrible and utterly disinterested high school student before I enlisted in the Marine Corps. I served four years, and eventually ended up enrolling in a community college upon leaving active duty.

As it turns out, I was no longer the student that I was in high school. I worked full-time while I attended classes, and I felt strangely out of place as an older, more experienced student, but I enjoyed college from the first day. And I did well.

After community college, I attended the University of Pittsburgh – a top quality research university. I started with philosophy – a subject in which Pitt is renowned – and I went on to learn about history, psychology, romance languages, and medieval studies. Most Pitt students do not need to write grand theses, but I earned a special degree through the University Honors College that required me to write, and publicly defend, an 80-page thesis. I wrote about the use of the word "substance" in metaphysics; I gave a public talk on the topic; and I survived an oral examination conducted by four accomplished philosophers. I participated in a special fellowship program one summer in which students pursued individual research projects. One of my peers studied geological formations in eastern Ohio; another considered correlations between inner city traffic and reported violent crimes. I researched the effects of English Common Law on women between the years 1400 and 1600. I earned admission to *Phi Beta Kappa* and graduated with high honors, but I was still thirsty for knowledge and challenges.

I took my degree at Pitt and leveraged that experience to pursue my dream: I went on to study at Ivy League schools. Several of them. I earned advanced degrees; I participated in a variety of academic, professional, and social activities; and I met some of the smartest, most driven people I have ever encountered.

I loved being a student. I loved the choice and the challenge. I could take any class I wanted. I could take easy courses or difficult courses, courses that tested by exams or by final papers. I appreciated the flexibility, depth, and breadth of my studies.

The funny thing is that, despite all of my education, I feel like I missed something. I never had *the* student experience. I was always a few years older than my peers. I worked and socialized outside of the university community. I was a commuter student, and college was not the central part of my life.

I also missed undergraduate life at the more elite universities. I am not regretful of my choices. I like blazing my own trail, creating unique opportunities, and leaving cartoonish, man-shaped holes in the wall when I leave a room – but my choices have left me wondering what the grass looks like in my well-educated neighbor's yard.

*

One summer day, I was looking at Brown University's Web site, and it occurred to me that I had never visited the campus. I had a wealth of knowledge about the university, but I had no idea what the air smelled like, whether Rhode Island was welcoming, or what activities students pursued on a Thursday night.

The more I thought about it, the more questions I had about the Ivies. I knew that Penn had a strong Greek (i.e. fraternity and sorority) scene, but I had never been to a frat party. I knew that Dartmouth was surrounded by forest, but I did not know if the students often wandered into it. Despite time spent at Cornell, I had never seen the inside of undergraduate student housing – in fact, I wasn't sure where all of the students lived. I did not know where

12

people at Harvard studied or what students at Columbia did for fun.

The idea for this project began to form in my mind. I could visit all eight schools for about a month each. I could be on campus when the freshmen arrived in August and attend graduation with the seniors in May. I would sit in on classes, talk with students, and see the sights. I would see what life at an Ivy is like for an undergraduate student. I would share my experiences of these exclusive institutions and the superstars who walk the campuses with the general public.

Of course, a scientific study would be painfully dull, if not impossible. I had very little interest in gathering and recounting statistics. Besides, I was too old in my thirties to actually blend into the undergraduate student body to gather information inconspicuously. It would be counterproductive and time consuming for me to try to edit out my own viewpoint from every observation to arrive at objective conclusions.

So I went a different route. I decided that I would embrace my subjectivity. I would experience and observe the schools through my own eyes, and I would recount those experiences and observations. The project would not be about the lives of college students, but rather about the life of one odd person observing the lives of college students. I would not need to worry about telling the "whole" story or relating what life was like for every student at all times – my story, for the purposes of this project, would *be* the "whole" story. Thus, I opted to abandon science in favor of a tale about my adventures.

Thus, I began. In late August, I packed a large suitcase, hopped in my car, and headed off to college. This is what I learned along the way.

The Things I Learned in College

CORNELL UNIVERSITY

Q: How many Cornell students does it take to screw in a light bulb?

A: Two – one to change the light bulb and one to crack under the pressure.

"Cornell is the easiest Ivy to get into and the hardest to get out of."

I heard that quote from dozens of students across the Cornell campus. It is a mantra that Cornellians hold dear.

They say that it is the easiest to get into because it admits more students than any other Ivy. The seven undergraduate schools and colleges enroll more than 13,000 students each year – a giant among the Ivies. It accepts applicants at a higher rate than its peers, but it is all about context: Cornell still turns away five prospective students for every one it admits.

Once a student makes it into Cornell, then the work begins. Grade inflation is minimal at Cornell, especially compared with some other Ivies, according to popular legend. Thus, an A is earned and an F is possible. The coursework at Cornell is exceptionally rigorous, and "fluff" courses are few and far between.

As a result, Cornell students are stereotyped as stressed out, neurotic nerds.

*

Cornell University has several notable distinctions in addition to being the largest Ivy. It is located in Ithaca, New York, marking the western border of the Ivies. With a founding date of 1865, it is also the youngest of the Ivies.

And, to me, it feels like home.

I am not exactly risk averse. I welcome challenges and I embrace trying circumstances. Where others might turn and run, I plod doggedly forward.

Nevertheless, when it came time to plot my course through the wilds of the Ivy League, I decided to start in a place that felt comfortable. I attended law school at Cornell, graduating just a year before I started this project. I had friends with whom I could live, contacts in the community that could introduce me to students, and a sense of the geography.

As it turned out, I made a great choice. When I contacted the first four Ivies on my schedule, Cornell was the quickest to respond. The director of the Cornell News Service reached out to me directly, asking a few questions about the project and my needs. It just so happened that I would be on campus less than a week later, and we arranged a meeting.

She took me to lunch at Banfi's, the upscale restaurant at the Statler Hotel on campus. The restaurant and hotel are integral to the campus, serving as an experiential piece of the education in the prestigious School of Hotel Administration.

Over lunch, she introduced me to various key administrators, including the director of Campus Information and Visitor Relations and the Dean of Students. Everyone had questions, which I answered to the best of my abilities.

"What's the theme of the book?"

I explained what I was doing.

"You know," one of the administrators began, "we are fiercely protective of our students..."

"I will absolutely protect the privacy of students," I assured the group. "They will not be identified, even if they want to be."

"What happens if a student tries to commit suicide while you're here?" another administrator inquired. "Will you write about it?"

16

It was a sensitive question and one that I had considered. Cornell has a reputation for people – not necessarily students – committing suicide. On a campus strewn with deep gorges straddled by bridges, people are occasionally driven by depression, insanity, curiosity, or drunkenness to jump. It does not do much to contradict Cornell's reputation as a place of stress.

"It will only be a subject if people are talking about it," I told them. They were the first people on campus to talk about it. Over the next month, several students, faculty members, and administrators made references to suicides on campus. It was certainly an issue – almost a piece of Cornell's legend – on the minds of the people I met. But, to the best of my knowledge, Cornell had no suicide attempts during my stay.

"Well," the director of the News Service said with a shrug, "we consider ourselves to be an open campus, and you are welcome here. We just want you to protect the privacy of our students."

Just like that, they welcomed me to campus and offered to help me as much as they could.

It was late summer, and I was at Cornell.

*

The entry to the Cornell campus from the north, which was my usual path, is unremarkable. I walked down a quiet residential street lined with trees and houses filled with character. Rounding a bend in the road, I found a small, brown sign announcing that I was entering Cornell University. No walls and no gates on this part of campus – just a continuation of the same street.

The houses, however, change. They become sororities, cooperative living units, and residential halls. The living environment of North Campus is all around.

The physical connection between North Campus and Central Campus is a bridge that spans one of the most impressive gorges in Ithaca. An angry waterfall feeds a stream that flows a couple hundred feet below the bridge. The gorge walls rise at 90-degree angles. In the summer months, you might find a few people splashing and sunning in the water, oblivious to the bustle of activity above them. It is easy, walking above them, to get a bit jealous – and a bit dizzy.

Once across the bridge, I entered the campus-proper. To the left on a hill is the Biochemistry Building – the first in a row of scientific laboratory and classroom buildings.

Heading to the right instead, I followed a footpath onto the Arts and Sciences Quadrangle. This is the oldest part of the campus, with a cornerstone on McGraw Hall that reads, in part, "Ezra Cornell, Chairman of the Board of Trustees, and A.D. White, President of the University."

A statue of A.D White rests in front of Goldwin Smith Hall, with its hefty white pillars and Greek revival architecture. Approximately 50 yards away beside Morrill Hall, with its Ivy-covered gray stone walls, sits a statue of Ezra Cornell. The monuments depicting these two famous Cornellians face each other. Painted footprints on the cement walkway, courtesy of the local fraternities, span the space between them. These footprints speak to the legend that if a virgin were to walk across the campus at the stroke of midnight as the carillon chimes played, the two statues would rise up, walk to the center of the quad, and shake hands.

Fortunately for the reputations of Cornell's students, noise ordinances in the City of Ithaca required that the chimes ring for the last time at 11:58 p.m.

Standing between these statues and looking back across the quad, I could see the old, shaded buildings of the College of Art, Architecture, and Planning, with the white dome of Sibley Hall peeking through the trees. The Johnson Art Museum – designed by I.M. Pei and looking to me like a mammoth, upright sewing machine – lay partially hidden by the trees and buildings at the edge of the scene.

Standing at the mouth of the quad sits perhaps the most iconic landmark of Cornell University: The Jennie McGraw Tower. Its four-faced clock can be seen atop the hill, and the sound of the carillon bells can be heard across the area.

The Tower received national attention on October 8, 1997. That was the day that the Cornell community awoke to find a gigantic pumpkin at the pinnacle of the roof. No one took credit for the caper, which defied explanation. Some speculated that a wealthy Cornellian employed a helicopter to pull off the prank; others thought that a team of students using one talented rock climber and a pulley system were responsible. In any case, the media photographed it for fluff stories around the country.

Several months passed before folks began to worry about the monstrous, frozen gourd looming above their heads. The university constructed a plan to remove the pumpkin. Friday, March 13, 1998, was planned as the day of execution. Classes were cancelled, and the community prepared for a day of live bands and free food.

The morning of the event, however, a gust of wind caused the crane-hoisted basket to bump the pumpkin during a practice run. The pumpkin toppled from its perch unceremoniously.

The pumpkin was more than an icon – it was a learning tool. Physics professors and students calculated the mechanics behind the pumpkin's descent; engineers used weather balloons to take small tissue samples from the fruit; and eventually Cornell scientists "autopsied" the pumpkin to discover that, yes, it was a pumpkin.

Today, postcards showing the McGraw Tower capped with the gourd are available on campus. For closer observation, a piece of the pumpkin is preserved in the world's preeminent human brain collection in Uris Hall on campus.

The Things I Learned in College

On one of my first days of this project, I walked past the Tower and followed the sidewalk down to Ho Plaza. The plaza is a major thoroughfare for students, with the university student union in Willard Straight Hall on one side, and the Campus Store on the other. Young men and women were using colorful, fat sticks of chalk to announce upcoming events on the walkway, and the plaza was lined with transient booths occupied by local banks vying for new students' checking accounts.

I saw the Peace Tower of the Law School at Myron Taylor Hall rising up before me as the chimes in the McGraw Tower behind me began to ring, signifying the changing of the hour.

I sighed, intoxicated by the environment, and turned left towards Day Hall – the main, administrative building where the free, student-led tours meet.

My tour guide was Heather, a senior in the Hotel School, and she spoiled me. I learned more facts in a couple of hours than I could have learned in a week of independent research. More importantly, I listened to a total stranger enthusiastically and competently discuss an Ivy League school. If people had questions, Heather had answers. She seemed to like her job, which struck me as harder than I would have guessed. She recited trivia by script and in response to queries, at the top of her lungs, while walking backwards over rough terrain and navigating around obstacles.

The tour lasted for an hour and a half, and it covered only a fraction of the campus. Heather and I were joined by a group of 18 parents and prospective students. The kids on the tour were extremely quiet, leaving the questioning exclusively to their parents. I, for my part, had the discipline to wait until after the tour before approaching Heather with my long list of questions.

It turned out that Heather was a very good sport. She answered my questions that day, she answered my questions when I bumped into her at Wegman's grocery store, she answered my questions when I met with a group of students that she was in, and she continued to answer my questions via email for months after I left Ithaca. She introduced me to her friends, and she invited me to her classes.

Without Heather and students like her, my project would have stalled.

*

Cornell is odd in its composition of colleges and schools. The undergraduate portion of the university consists of seven undergraduate schools and colleges. The distinction between colleges and schools is that the former offers multiple majors and the latter have only one available major. Four of these institutions – the College of Arts and Sciences; the College of Engineering; the School of Hotel Administration; and the College of Art, Architecture, and Planning – are private schools. Three of the undergraduate colleges and schools – the College of Human Ecology; the College of Agriculture and Life Sciences; and the School of Industrial and Labor Relations – are supported in part by a contract with the State of New York.

Cornell's relationship with the State of New York dates back to the Morrill Land-Grant Act of 1862. Abraham Lincoln designated one school in each state as Land-Grant institutions. Cornell is the only Ivy that is also its state's Land-Grant school. In the case of Cornell, the deeded land was in the Midwest, so the property was sold and the money was invested in the university.

The colleges and schools on state contract often confuse people. The courses are rigorous, and admissions are selective. Students in all of the various colleges and schools live and socialize together, and the classes of each unit are generally open to all undergraduates. The difference is chiefly financial – students who are residents of the State of New York and who attend a state-supported school at Cornell pay a reduced tuition rate.

As I talked with undergrads, I discovered a strange pecking order among the schools.

When I asked an Agriculture and Life Sciences student (or "Aggie") what students in Arts and Sciences thought of the school, he said, "They think that they are better than us because we go to a state school."

When I asked an Arts and Sciences student what the students in the Ag School thought of his school, he said, "They think we're snobs who think that we are better than they are."

Agriculture and Life Sciences students referred to Arts and Sciences students as "Arts and Crafts" students. Arts and Sciences students refer to Ag students as "Farmers."

Students in the Hotel School told me, "Other students think we party all of the time."

Granted, I was told this at a Hotelie party on a Tuesday evening.

Ask a Human Ecology student what others think of them, and they say, "Nothing. No one knows anything about our school."

In this case, they are pretty much right. The College of Human Ecology basically studies "the human condition." The college offers majors such as Human Development, Nutritional Science, and Textiles and Apparel. It is a small school, a descendent of the old Home Economics program at Cornell.

Art, Architecture, and Planning (AAP) students supposedly have a rivalry with Engineers and vice versa, hence one of the school's greatest traditions spawned by one of the school's greatest heroes: Willard Straight.

Straight, a member of the class of 1901, was an architecture student at Cornell before the birth of the College of Art, Architecture, and Planning. He was not an academic powerhouse, but he had a reputation as a Big

22

Man on Campus. His influence on the school during his tenure was strictly social.

According to the legend, Straight had two goals in life. He wanted to become very rich, and he wanted to marry a very beautiful woman. Cleverly, he married a very rich and beautiful woman.

When he died in World War I, Straight left a financial gift to the university. His gift, however, came with an unusual stipulation. The money, according to the legend, could not be used for any academic purpose. Eventually, the money was used to design and build Willard Straight Hall. Today, the building houses the student union with various shops, student activities offices, a movie theatre, and dining areas. In the late 1960s, the union became the subject of national attention when radical students bearing firearms took it over until the administration met their demands. To reduce the threat of future takeovers, the administration allowed a bank to open an office in the building, making any takeover a federal offense.

Straight, however, received his wish: The building has no classrooms or academic space. He also, according to lore, received another wish. The great room, named Memorial Hall, is lined with wooden buttresses along the ceiling. Each buttress is carved with a human figure, but close examination reveals that they are each very different. The images on the right side of the room are likenesses of the professors that Straight liked and admired during his time at Cornell. The carvings are of wise men reading, deep in thought, or writing. On the left are the replicas of the professors that Straight disliked. The carvings depict men picking their noses, pulling out their hair, or sticking out their tongues.

That Willard was a funny guy.

The campus is full of Willard Straight stories and legends. But one popular tradition started by Straight is Dragon Day.

Each spring, the first-year architecture undergrads build a Dragon. The Dragon is between 40 and 60 feet long, and it is always different. The creativity and resourcefulness of the students cannot be overestimated. The creations are beautiful and frightening, sometimes breathing fire and sometimes roaring with sound.

The freshmen architects gather under the Dragon and walk it around campus on or around St. Patrick's Day. When it returns to the Arts Quad, which is lovingly decorated with toilet paper and signs, the fifth-year architecture students – staying at Cornell the additional year to earn the professional Bachelor of Architecture degree – light the Dragon on fire. Nine times out of ten, the freshmen have emerged from under the Dragon before it is set ablaze.

But in the Dragon's travels, it runs past the Engineering Quad.

Engineers hate the Dragon and the Dragon hates Engineers – it is a rivalry between the people who design buildings and the people who make them stand. Engineers line up to pelt the Dragon with toilet paper, snowballs, graphing calculators, or anything else they can get their hands on.

I did not find anyone on either side of the rivalry who was passionate about it. I met Architecture students who were passionate about building or burning a Dragon, and I met Engineers who were passionate about throwing stuff. But the rivalry behind the tradition was minimal. Instead, most of the engineers and AAP students who I met felt more of a rivalry with the College of Arts and Sciences.

One of the strangest things that I encountered was a sense of inferiority at Cornell. The fact that Cornell admitted more students than any other Ivy was not lost on the student population. Many of the students that I met received rejections from Harvard, Yale, or Princeton during the admissions process. They felt that on the Ivy League food chain, they were at the bottom, partially because of the fact that Cornell shared its Ivy League reputation with the state contract schools.

After a class, a guy approached me about the book. He asked, "Are you going to address the people who think that Cornell isn't really an Ivy League school?"

I was at a loss for what to say. I replied that Cornell is, by definition, an Ivy League school – it plays in the Ivy League football conference – and anyone who reads my book should walk away knowing that. He, a Cornell student, seemed unconvinced.

Another student told me the story of his friend who earned admission to Cornell and to the State University of New York (SUNY) at Binghamton. The financial aid package at Binghamton was too good to pass up, and she decided to forego her offer at Cornell. Her friend said, "But this is Cornell! You can't pass up a chance to go to the Ivy League!"

And she responded, "I'd rather go to the Ivy of the SUNY schools than the SUNY of the Ivy schools."

That is not to say that the students were unhappy. In fact, I did not meet a single student who claimed to be disappointed in his or her decision to attend Cornell. Some students wished for beaches and some longed for the big city, but everyone expressed happiness that they were living and learning at Cornell.

But it did not stop them from joking. As one student told me at about 2 a.m., working on a project in Rand Hall, "Going to Cornell is like having unprotected sex: You are glad you got in, but you are sorry you came."

*

On my way to my car one day, I passed a woman riding a bicycle. Ithaca is an art town with an active farmer's market, and it attracts many organic, "crunchy" people. This woman may have been one of those people. On the other hand, she may have been homeless.

She wore a long tan skirt and an orange hazard vest with an American flag on the back. For a helmet, she wore something that resembled a spaghetti colander. Her legs pumped furiously on the pedals, creating a breeze that tossed the strands of stringy, gray hair that fell from under her strainer.

As she blew past me, she looked at my red Cornell T-shirt – not exactly out of place in Ithaca – and she whooped, "Yeah, Cornell!"

Apparently, I am not the only college freak.

*

The undergrads at Cornell were attractive, and they knew it. They were not necessarily vain, but several students commented to me that they noticed – and were surprised by – how good-looking the other students were.

It could not be denied. Beauty may be subjective, but it would take one odd subject not to find the beautiful people wandering the campus.

I asked a few students their opinions on the personal aesthetics at Cornell, and overwhelmingly received a single explanation from them: The geography of the campus.

Students seemed to believe that the beauty came from the amount of exercise that they received just walking from their living spaces to their classes. The campus is not flat, and it can take more than 15 minutes to walk across it.

I was not sure that the terrain was really the key factor. I spent some time in the dining halls, and – more to the point – I spent some time in the wee hours at Louie's Lunch on North Campus. It would take one heck of a walk to counterbalance Louie's grilled ham and cheese. Besides, the only lines longer than those at Louie's food

26

truck at 2 a.m. were those for the buses to carry students three quarters of a mile to their dorms.

On the other hand, I was very impressed with the level of athletics that I saw on campus. The university has weight rooms and cardio equipment, and most of the students I met joined the gyms. Of course, it was September, and fitness resolve may have trickled away as the year wore on.

I also met many people involved in sports. I met people who played varsity football and many people who just played football after classes. I met a member of Cornell's competitive Ultimate Frisbee team, and everywhere I looked I saw people playing Frisbee. I met a woman on the fencing team, and I witnessed a mock duel between two young men with sticks in a gorge. People exercised all over campus.

I met a girl named Olivia at a party, and she mentioned that she was a runner. When I suggested that we run together, she had one question.

"Are you fast?" she asked.

I smiled and responded, "No."

It was an honest answer. For all of my running, I am pathetically slow. I can run decent distances – and I can do it in boots while wearing a backpack and carrying a rifle, if that were ever necessary – but I don't expect to see eight-minute miles again in my life. My little brother, Jason, still on active duty in the Marines, sometimes takes me running with him. He runs at least as far as I do; he can carry twice as much weight and an anti-tank missile launcher; and he can do it wearing boots that are so big that the Marine Corps needed to special order them when the freak showed up at Boot Camp. All that, and he is working his way towards six-minute miles. My struggling to keep up amuses him.

Olivia suggested that we run together the next day at 8 a.m. Right there, she set herself apart from the masses of students who would hate to do anything that early in the morning.

We met in College Town and took off on foot. Within the first few steps, I realized the errors that I had committed: 1) I did not ask her if *she* was fast, and 2) I did not define how fast is fast. She boogied up the streets as I struggled to keep pace. Somehow, I was hanging in and able to hold up my end of the conversation.

Then the other shoe dropped. She hung a right and darted into the woods. I was suddenly on a narrow footpath, going up and down steep rises, and leaping over roots, rocks, and fallen branches. As we went past Six-mile Creek – a spot that I had never seen previously – she told me that students hang out there, swimming in the water during the warm months. It looked inviting, but Olivia was off again, and I trotted after her.

I only fell twice before we reached the road again and I pulled up beside her. We had ceased chatting during our time on the multi-mile trail, because we had to run single file and, of course, because it was important that I breathe as I negotiated obstacles. On the road again, we picked up the conversation where we had left off with her sharing her thoughts on life at Cornell.

I was doing okay when I questioned how much farther she planned on running. She pointed ahead and said, "We just need to go up there and then we're done."

She was pointing straight up Buffalo Street.

Buffalo Street is what daring kids conjure to mind when they think of sled riding; it is the place where paranoid, and even reasonable, people fear that the brakes in their cars will give out. It is approximately half a mile long and rises at an impossible angle. Only once in my years at Cornell had I run up Buffalo Street, and there was a moment during the slow assent that I realized I was actually drifting backwards.

"Yeah, good luck with that," I muttered shifting to a walk.

She was very gracious – much more so than Jason would have been. He would have just picked me up and tossed me over his shoulder while calling me a baby and continuing the run. Olivia simply bounded up the hill without me.

*

Every student at Cornell is required to take a swimming test. It is the first test that they take at Cornell, occurring during freshman orientation. It is pretty simple: Students have to travel the length of the 25-yard pool three times – once on their fronts, once on their backs, and once however they can manage. Those who fail need to sign up for a swimming course at Cornell – a course that satisfies a distribution requirement needed for graduation – or petition for an exception to the rule. Thus, the stakes are not exceptionally high.

I heard several students speculate about why Cornell has a swim test. I heard that Abraham Lincoln insisted upon a swim test as a part of the Morrill Land-Grant because he wanted to produce Union soldiers who would be able to swim. I heard that the State of New York had a regulation that dictated that all college graduates be able to swim. I heard that Willard Straight liked swimming, so everyone at Cornell should too.

One of the more interesting explanations that I heard was that the swimming test was the result of an alumni donation. A wealthy graduate had a son or daughter who had drowned, so the graduate made a gift on the condition that Cornell students learn how to avoid the same fate.

The "donation" story is actually a myth passed down from class to class. The same campus legend can be found at other colleges and universities around the country, but particularly at schools in New York such as Hamilton, Colgate, and Columbia that require all students to pass a

29

swim test. One popular version of the myth involves Eleanor Elkins Widener. Ms. Widener donated the money for the Widener Library at Harvard in honor of her son, a Harvard alumnus who died with his father aboard the *Titanic*. The legend says that she donated money to the school contingent upon the creation of a swim test so that graduates would not die at sea. Of course, it would take a heck of a swim test to get people ready to swim in freezing water 400 miles to the nearest landmass.

In fact, around and after the time of World War I, the Red Cross launched a campaign to encourage people to learn how to swim. Over the years, many schools picked up the cause and began teaching and requiring that skill. Cornell adopted its swimming requirement in the 1940s during World War II. The policy is still reviewed periodically and voted on by the faculty, but Cornell remains committed to a floating and swimming student body.

The swim tests are amusing to watch, and not because every year at least someone who has never tried to swim previously steps into the pool and sinks hopelessly to the bottom. The students for the most part embrace the test, and they dress for it. The undergraduates take their tests at opposite ends of the campus – the men at the Teagle Pool and the women at the Helen Newman Pool – and they walk in droves to these locations. On the days of the swimming test, I saw groups of kids walking in bathrobes and slippers, carrying everything from snorkel gear to floatation devices to rubber duckies.

The swim test is only required for undergraduates at Cornell. Had I been required to swim three laps on my way into law school, however, I would have been fine.

I swim better than I run – and I swim better than Jason, despite his flipper-like feet. On a hot day, I looked for an opportunity to take advantage of the natural geography of the Cornell campus.

I waded into the water of Beebe Lake – which is really too small to be called a lake – at about five o'clock in the afternoon on a Tuesday in September. The water was a comfortable temperature and relatively clean.

I swam under a bridge that I had watched students jump off of – about 25 feet above the surface of the water – and continued upstream into the gorge. The steep rock walls of the gorge lined both sides of the waterway. The water flowed in a stream that was about fifteen feet across. The bottom was too deep to comfortably touch, and I'm not the kind of guy to go searching with hands or feet for the depths of a body of water when I cannot see what I'm touching. Near the sides of the gorge, I found places where I could temporarily stand, but the ledges were narrow.

I slowly swam about 100 meters or so upstream, watching the gorge. I was alone, although I could hear a couple of people talking to each other on one of the overlooks, unaware of my presence. The gorge meandered around several turns before I saw my goal.

Directly upstream was a waterfall. It was not the most magnificent that I had seen on campus. In fact, if I were to hold perfectly still and allow the water to carry me back to Beebe Lake and across it, I would have been swept into *the* campus waterfall, visible from the bridge between central campus and north campus. This waterfall, however, was impressive because of my vantage point. It was a multi-tiered affair, making a rush of noise and pushing the current against me.

When I reached the falls, I swam beneath them for a bit. I thought about how odd it was that I had spent three years at Cornell and had never even known this particular geologic feature existed, and I wondered how many students would leave without this experience.

*

31

I attended my first fraternity party ever, several weeks into my stay at Cornell.

I had been a student for more than a decade, but I didn't think it was odd that I had never attended a frat party. I was not in a fraternity, and I really did not have any desire to be in one, so why would I go to a frat party?

The undergrads at Cornell were amazed that I had never engaged in Greek life at all, including attending any parties. Indeed, I did not meet anyone – counting freshmen who had only been on campus for a week or so – who had not already had the experience.

The reason for the surprise is because Greek life includes most people at Cornell at some point. Approximately 30% of the student body is a member of a fraternity or sorority, making Cornell one of the biggest Greek systems in the country, but it is also a part of the freshman experience. On weekends, fraternities throw parties as informal recruitment events, and freshmen wander from party to party with their friends and peers from their residence halls.

In fact, I learned something as I spoke to students about Greek life. When I asked juniors and seniors if they belonged to a fraternity or sorority, I found that there were two large groups. Half the people I asked responded, "Yeah, and it's great," and the other half rolled their eyes or looked offended as they said, "No, I'm not one of *them*."

Of the dozens and dozens of freshmen to whom I posed the question of whether they planned to enter Greek life, *every single one of them* stated with resolve, "Yes."

My first party was an unregistered, unofficial party. In fact, it was a fraternity party not technically held in a fraternity house. The fraternity was officially dry, so no alcohol was allowed in the house. Cleverly, but transparently, they rented an apartment less than 200 yards away where they could drink all they liked.

The party served plenty of beer to masses of Cornell undergrads, traveling in large packs from party to party.

The sheer sea of students flowing into and out of the party was breathtaking. At one point, I found myself pinned in the flow of traffic on an old wooden porch. Just me and about 60 of my closest friends stuck on a piece of rotten wood designed to hold about a dozen people a couple of stories in the air.

My interactions with the party attendees were minimal. They thought I was security, and I thought they were too young to approach. I was considering leaving when I had my only real conversation of the evening.

A young girl was making her way through the line on the porch leading into the apartment. She was talking with everyone around her and bouncing to the music emanating from the house. She was the most intoxicated person I had seen that night, judging by her motor control and smell.

As she reached me, she stumbled and fell forward. In an effort to catch herself, she reached out and grabbed, hooking her hand through a small silver chain I wear around my neck.

I awkwardly tried to support her while preventing her from breaking my necklace. Once I disentangled her, she swayed back a step, pointed at the cross hanging on my chain, and said, "That's *so* cool!" Then she held her hand up, palm facing me.

I knew what she wanted. She wanted me to give her a high-five.

I make it a general practice not to partake in high-fives. For me, it is extremely artificial because I am not a high-five-kind-of-guy. I firmly believe that high-fives are what happens when meaningless elevator small talk deteriorates to hand gestures.

But I was a guest, and in the name of research, I gave her a high-five.

She was invigorated by the gesture. "All right!" she hollered. Then she asked me in a serious tone, "Your cross: It's for Jesus?"

I was honestly confused by the question. "No, it's mine."

She looked at me intensely, soberly. "Man, I saw his *face!*"

Then the crowd surged forward and she was gone, jammed through the doorway. I never saw her again.

But I was not done with Greek life at Cornell. The brothers of one of the largest and most popular fraternities on campus invited me to their annual "Green Party."

The first fraternity party was different from how I imagined it would be. It was hundreds of impossibly young people wandering through to drink some beer before moving on to the next party. All I knew about fraternity parties was what I saw in movies. I expected to find dancing, games, a theme – some kind of organization.

I found it all at the Green Party.

I stopped by the house during the afternoon on the day of the party as the brothers were setting up. The brothers spent the daylight hours cutting and collecting limbs from trees and using them to turn the inside of their house into a woodland dance hall, hence the name. Boughs hung on every wall and from every ceiling beam. A 20-foot birch tree sat in the middle of the stairwell, resting on the ground floor and rising above the first floor landing. Mike, my guide, told me that the tree was found on the other side of Ithaca and brought in strapped to the roof of a Jeep Wrangler.

Mike also told me that the brothers had accidentally invaded the Cornell Plantation – a planned wildlife section of the campus – and had been caught by the Cornell Police Department removing limbs from trees. The brothers had been issued a citation, and they would need to appear before various administrative groups, including possibly the Cornell Judicial Administrator and the Inter Fraternity Council. Mike was not sure what punishments would result from the offense – it was an unusual act – but he assumed it would involve community service and possibly probation.

Greek organizations often have periods of probation for violations. The first time someone mentioned that their fraternity was on probation, I felt a bit guilty for bringing it up, and I changed the subject to spare him from rehashing the traumatic incident. After speaking to many more Greeks, I realized that although not every fraternity suffered probation, the ones who *do* anything did. An unregistered party, underage drinking, and maybe even pruning the wrong trees could lead to probation. The reason why sororities tend to avoid probation is because they do not host parties, so they do not incur violations punishable by probation as often, nor would they be as hurt by a period of probation wherein they could not throw parties. The Greek community seems numb to the punishment.

In any case, the threat of probation was not slowing the brothers of this fraternity down. They decorated the house as Mike showed me around.

The house was a mansion. It had a large dining area that served as a woodsy dance floor with a stage for a live band during parties. Upstairs, a large room called the Great Hall, would hold a DJ and second dance floor. The brothers were not decorating the living areas that could house as many as 55 people.

Later in the day, I attended a security briefing with the brothers. The Green Party, unlike my previous experience at a fraternity party, was registered with the university. It was too big and too popular to hide. The fraternity expected more than 1,000 guests to pass through the house over the course of the evening.

The brothers gathered in front of the stage on the ground floor around a large container of Buffalo wings. Mike, who was overseeing security for the night, led the meeting.

He handed out lists to the other young men. "These are the shifts for the night: Two brothers in the parking lot, two at the front door as usual, and then the fire alarms and side doors. Anyone have any questions?"

Party guests sometimes pull fire alarms when they are drunk, so brothers guard the alarms throughout the house.

Mike went on, "If you are on the sober list, stay relatively sober. We aren't going to be driving anyone anywhere tonight, so nobody has to be dead sober, but stay reasonable."

Vince, the fraternity's president, spoke up, "Actually, let me just say one thing. You can have a good time without blacking out. Take your time tonight. If your goal is to black out, why not wait until midnight to get rolling? We can use some sober people earlier in the night."

"Where's Rick?" Mike asked.

"He's still spraying the leaves upstairs," someone volunteered. "He's almost done."

The previous year, the fraternity paid to have Rick, one of their brothers, certified by the Ithaca Fire Department as a fire safety specialist. He was instructed on how to fireproof the leaves of the boughs that were brought into the house. I saw him earlier working with a spray bottle carefully dousing each leaf with a fire retardant. I was told that a fire inspector arrived last year during the height of the party, picked a leaf from the wall, and held a lighter to it. When it did not ignite, he turned and left the party unmolested.

"We hired security for the night. I think they are bringing six guys with them," Mike continued. "Where do we want to put them?"

The brothers debated strategies before settling on locations. The biggest debate was whether or not to post security to block the hallways leading to bedrooms, and if

36

they did, how the brothers could get past security if they wanted to.

The B.Y.O.B. policy stated that the fraternity could not supply any alcohol, and that each guest had to bring their own. According to Mike, nobody in their right mind could expect to throw a successful B.Y.O.B. party on this scale. As Mike explained this to me, he showed me the walk-in refrigerator that was stocked with 120 cases of beer.

To game the system, a brother had ripped handfuls of carnival tickets and placed them beside the bars, so at a glance it would seem that they were collecting tickets in exchange for beer.

Mike printed out a fake guest list that was about three years old and placed it at the front door. He figured that the token gestures to meet the university's guidelines, plus the sincere effort of protecting the safety and security of his guests, would ensure a successful party.

The guest list turned out to be the problem.

By 11 o'clock, the place was the epitome of a fraternity party. The music was thumping through the first floor of the house, and the dance floor was packed with young men in jeans and collared shirts, and women in short skirts and low tops. The room was dark, save the lasers and strobe lights refracting off of the leaves. Traffic inched along at the margins of the party. Those perseverant enough to navigate the first floor made it to the stairs heading to the basement. In the dining room, the dance floor was less crowded because the band had not yet arrived. Music blared through speakers, and people danced on the floor and on the stage, while a handful of young women jockeyed for turns to swing on the two stripper poles installed for the party. Beer was everywhere, and the house was alive.

Outside, a frenzied mob of freshmen crowded in the parking lot and yard. Groups of freshmen walked down the long drive, leaving the party, shouting to their peers heading up the driveway, "Don't even try it! You'll never get in!"

Around that time, the Cornell Police arrived on the scene. The first officer through the door looked like a caricature of a small town policeman. His gut fell over his gun belt, and he had a thin regulation moustache.

Inside the front door, the officer asked the security guard for the guest list. The security guard looked to the brother stationed at the door. The brother went off to find the guest list that had somehow been moved from the front door where the rules stated that it had to be.

That was all the officer needed. He stepped into the room and looked around. He approached a kid with a beer in his hand and demanded ID. He examined the ID with a flashlight and reluctantly let the kid pass. He grabbed a second kid and demanded his ID. When the kid admitted that he did not have any ID with him, the officer headed for the DJ's booth and told the DJ to shut down the music. The brothers spoke with the officers, but it was over. After only two hours, the party was shut down.

Thus, the hours spent preparing for the party, the thousands of dollars that went to security and the band, and the hassle of arranging a registered party were lost.

The guests began clearing out as the brothers and their closest friends talked about what they were going to do for the rest of the night. Several brothers apologized to me, embarrassed that I witnessed the debacle. One of the people who felt the worst was Kevin.

Kevin was a junior in the College of Arts and Sciences, and he was a brother in the house. He was a member of the Inter Fraternity Council, and he was eager to share all he knew about Greek life at Cornell.

He gave me a tour of the house. We went down into the now-defunct lower party room and ducked into the kitchen. It was an industrial affair, complete with a deep fryer – just what every growing boy needs in his life. The kitchen was open to all members of the fraternity, but it is also where a professional chef prepared 12 meals a week for the members. In addition, a brother was paid to prepare one meal a week, and another brother was paid to clean the dishes each night.

Kevin led me upstairs to the residential hall, navigating the occasional drunk student. He opened a door to a bedroom that he described as typical. It was larger than I expected, with a bed, desk, and television. In the daylight, the view from the window was of Ithaca and Cayuga Lake. I asked how much it cost to live in the house, and I received the same unlikely answer that I received from every brother or sister whom I asked: a few thousand dollars *less* than it cost to live in one of Cornell's dorms.

The tour ended on the deck. The wooden structure was affixed to the back of the house. It was built on the roof of the main floor, and could hold more than 300 people. Two picnic tables and many benches adorned the deck, and it was packed with people who did not want to leave the party, mostly brothers and their friends.

Ted, a Korean-American, joined Kevin and me on the deck. He began the conversation by apologizing that the party ended so early. Then he offered to cheer me up by chugging a beer.

He seemed to like to cheer people up.

Ted told me that he was the fastest drinker in the fraternity and, as one of the only Asian members, he wanted to create a stereotype of Asians as fast drinkers. Because I do not drink anything stronger than soda, I thought I would not be impressed by Ted's abilities, but I was wrong. He chugged against several other young men, beating them cleanly without a hint of fatigue.

Pleased with his abilities, he tried a second trick to impress me: beer pong, more commonly referred to as "Beirut" at Cornell. He and his partner, a freshman who had survived the exodus and was undergoing recruitment, stood at one end of a picnic table. They set 20 cups, each

1/3 full with beer, in two bowling pin formations on each side. They set another cup, this one filled with water, to the side. Their opponents, a young man and woman, had the same arrangement opposite them. They began throwing ping-pong balls across the table aiming for the cups. After every missed shot, they cleaned the ball in the water cup; after every hit, they chugged the cup of beer while the balls continued to fly.

Cornellians seemed to easily accept the name "Beirut" for the game, but it struck me as odd. Only months later did a friend explain the origin of the name. When played correctly, the ball should land in the cups like a bomb, and the game was named for the bombing of Beirut in the 1980s.

Ted tried to teach me the game, but I never quite got all of the rules. The brothers of this fraternity played with a set of rules named after their house, and to their knowledge, their house was the only place in the world where Beirut was played by these rules. I wanted to talk with other people on the deck, so I kept drifting away, only to have Ted place an arm around my shoulders and shepherd me back. Eventually, however, I made it away.

As I stood on the deck, a kid walked right up to me and said angrily, "Are you writing the book?"

I looked up at him. He was about seven feet tall, drunk, and very angry. "Err...Yeah?"

"You need to put this in," he stated clamping a hand on my shoulder tightly. "They can't do this to us!"

"Who?" I asked innocently.

The kid shook his head with exasperation. His other hand rose in a fist, and although he did not swing at me, I could see that he really wanted to. "The police. They can't just come in here. They are violating our constitutional rights. Article Four of the Bill of Rights protects, 'the right of people to be secure in their persons, houses, papers...'" Only at Cornell can you get beaten up by a drunken giant quoting the U.S. Constitution. "This is a house! They can't come in like they own the place!"

But, as a matter of fact, they do. The fraternity sold the house to the university to cover a multi-million dollar debt several years ago. Thus, the house was university-owned, and the police could enter.

But I was not about to debate constitutional law with Jethro.

Things were looking grim when Ted, my old buddy, came and hollered, "We just won! That's three games in a row! That has to go in your book!"

Anything to get back to the game!

I watched Ted win several more games and drink himself silly. At one point, with only one cup left before a seventh victory, he clutched on to me as a sign of love and to keep from falling over. He said, "S.M., if I make this shot, I get a quote in your book. Come on!"

"Okay," I agreed. "Make this next shot, and I'll give you four words."

The ball went off the table and under the railing, bouncing down into one of Ithaca's many gorges. We will never know what those four words would have been.

Over the course of the next three hours, I spoke with dozens of people. Some were fraternity brothers spending time in their house; some were young women, half of them flirting and playing, and the other half trying to stay awake and talk their flirting roommates into leaving; and some were freshmen, often saying, "I can't wait to rush this fraternity!"

There is more – too much more – to write.

My adventure included seeing Yolanda King in a student/professional production of *A Raisin in the Sun* with guest director Reggie Life. I went as the guest of perhaps the most beautiful woman I have ever met in real life, a student named Gwen. This sophomore was a double major, fluent in Italian, and active in a sorority. After the show, she took me to the sorority house – a mansion, really – and introduced me to her sisters.

They explained to me that the different sororities had different reputations. I was astonished to learn that theirs was not known as the most attractive girls – it seemed that the whole sorority of impossibly blonde women could ride on Gwen's coattails to that distinction. Nor were they the brainy girls, the slutty girls, or the athletic girls. They were the popular girls who received the first invitations to the best events – presumably beating even the slutty girls.

I had later opportunities to explore Greek life, but I will never forget that my first exposure was with the gracious students of Cornell. It is easy to take a person seen in one context and turn him or her into a caricature. These students, however, are complex, more thoughtful and talented than any caricature can express.

*

At Cornell, I spent at least an hour talking one-on-one or in small groups with several dozen students; I met and conversed with a few hundred more; and I observed a couple thousand students in class and at campus events. I now examine the stereotype of Cornell students as stressed out, neurotic nerds in light of my new perspective.

True, the students are under pressure. They are competing for good grades in an environment where their competition is just as bright and accomplished as they are. They work hard through many years of education to get to where they are, and they want to make the best of it.

The stress, however, is self-imposed. Students take on massive amounts of work. Double majors abound, and everyone seems to be involved in sports or activities. Many undergrads have lofty goals – such as attending prestigious graduate schools, running for political offices, or leading profitable business organizations – and they use their time at Cornell to prepare for future challenges.

If the students were especially stressed out, I could not tell. In fact, the only student that I met who seemed close to the proverbial edge was a freshman in his second week on campus. Granted, he was sitting by himself at a bus stop, hugging his knees and rocking back and forth as he told me, "It's too hard, man. It's just too hard." But he was unique in my experience. More seasoned students told tales of how they learned to manage their time and to prioritize. They said that they felt stressed at times, but they knew that they could handle it.

As for the label "nerds," Cornell students are anything but. The students at Cornell were some of the most attractive, well-rounded people I have met in my life. I found them to be athletic, concerned about the state of the world, interested in pop culture, and extremely human, both individually and as a class.

In mid-September, I prepared to leave Cornell for the next Ivy. I was comfortable at Cornell. I had just acquired a group of friends and found the best classes. I was nervous about the change, and entertaining thoughts of procrastination, but I was encouraged by my progress thus far. As I drove out of Ithaca towards Providence, Rhode Island, I thought to myself, "How bad can it be?"

The Things I Learned in College

BROWN UNIVERSITY

Q: How many Brown students does it take to screw in a light bulb?

A: Eleven – one to screw in the light bulb and ten to share the experience.

Brown University has a long-standing reputation as a liberal haven, almost a commune for ultra-smart and intensely-driven hippies. One of the most famous features of the school is its policy stating that students can take all of their classes on a pass/fail basis, and the university has no distribution requirements. Thus, an undergraduate can earn a degree without ever receiving a letter grade or taking a science course.

On a related note, the school also has a popular reputation for marijuana use.

It is also a place of feminism. It is famous for its orgasm and feminine sexuality seminars.

The bottom line is that if you are a brilliant liberal looking for love, education, and a place to play Hacky Sack, Brown may be your school.

*

"Why the fuck is your name 'Ivy League?'"

That was the message I received on the Daily Jolt, an electronic bulletin board and early social media platform used by the students at Brown. When I chose the pseudonym as a logon, it seemed like a good idea. In my second week on campus, I posted a query on the "Courses Forum," asking what the best classes were at the university. I received a few responses looking for more clarification – because, apparently, the term "best classes" was too vague without more detail – before I received the message above.

I think I handled the message with dignity. I posted a reply to the anonymous malcontent in which I explained that I am a big fan of the Ivy League and that I was at Brown writing a book about undergraduate life in the Ivies. Afterwards, several students helpfully posted some course names with no further assaults on me.

The message, however, is symbolic of my early experiences at Brown.

You might remember my conversation earlier with administrators over lunch at Cornell. I wrote to every school that I would visit, telling them about my project and asking them for whatever help they could lend.

Every institution responded differently. Cornell took me to lunch. Another school thanked me for letting them know about my visit. One Ivy offered to make some introductions to student groups or offices across campus. A couple of schools ignored me altogether.

Brown was not keen on helping me. They stopped short of disallowing my visit, but they denied my request for assistance and support. The e-mail I received from a senior administrator – I'll call him Mr. Smith – made it clear that help would not be forthcoming from the institution.

I responded to Smith and advised him that I would carry on with my project as scheduled. I said that I would contact him again while I was in town.

The next time I reached out to Mr. Smith was a week or so into my visit at Brown. I e-mailed him the day before an article about my project was scheduled to appear in the *Brown Daily Herald*. I wanted to warn him, because I knew that the university's reaction to my visit was bound to be a part of the article. In addition to letting him know about the article, I also apologized for not dropping by his office yet. I wrote that I hoped to meet him soon.

I immediately received the following terse response:

>You did say you'd check in when you got to town. The first I heard was when the BDH reporter called up.

That was it. No greeting, no signature.

I had heard nothing but wonderful things about Smith. A former editor-in-chief of the *Brown Daily Herald* told me Smith was very friendly and competent, and she could not believe that he refused my request for access. As I left Cornell, I wrote a thank you note to an administrator for her help, and in it I mentioned that Brown was not welcoming me. She immediately replied that I should just avoid whomever was giving me a problem at Brown and go straight to Mr. Smith. He would take care of me, she advised.

And, to be clear, I do not blame the school or Smith for being wary. I dreamed of assistance – for example, being allowed to live in a residence hall – but I knew it was a stretch. I can understand and appreciate why an institution might be skeptical about having me on campus. It makes sense.

It also made my life just a wee bit harder. I felt sneaky and sordid crashing the campus, and I was concerned about getting in trouble, but my journey was underway.

*

The first thing I needed to do on campus was to get an appreciation for the lay of the land. I figured my best shot was to take the official tour.

I went to the Admissions Office at Corliss Brackett Hall on Prospect Street to sign on for the tour. When I walked into the hall, which is more of a great house converted for university use, I encountered a desk manned by an older woman. Actually, and I hope this is not out of line, I think there comes a point where one can abandon political correctness and call a person old. This woman may have only been in her late nineties, but I doubted she had seen double digits on her birthday cards in a long time. She seemed to be semi-blind, mostly deaf, and very confused about why she was behind that desk.

"Hi," I said, walking up to the desk. She numbly tilted her head up at me. I asked, "Is this where the tours meet?"

She did not acknowledge that she heard me. I raised my voice and repeated the question. She croaked, "What do you want?"

"A tour!" I said, loudly.

"Yes," she replied simply, as if that settled the matter.

"Should I wait here?" I screamed.

"Wait for what?"

"A tour!" This time, I wiggled my fingers in the international sign of walking. I began to wonder if she would be leading the next tour.

She nodded slightly, indicating understanding, but all she said was, "No."

I was determined to wait her out this time. I stood perfectly still in front of her desk for several seconds. Eventually, she looked up at me and seemed surprised to see me there. She slowly pointed a bony finger towards a room off the reception area. The gesture seemed ominous, and I was mildly concerned that I had walked into a horror movie and she was sending me to the basement to meet her inbred, chainsaw-loving offspring.

Instead, I found myself in a beautiful waiting area with a fireplace and shelves of old, impressive looking books. A few other people sat in the deep, comfortable chairs, presumably waiting for the tour.

A young woman – a junior named Marla – walked in and announced that the tour was starting, and she directed us to all step outside. It was a beautiful day in September, with a cloudless blue sky and trees that were faintly highlighted with orange and red foliage. The temperature was comfortably warm as we set out.

The Brown campus is enthralling. Set in a hilltop neighborhood overlooking Providence, the campus is a combination of new and old buildings.

We walked up Prospect Street, passing residential houses on our right and left. We crossed a minor intersection at Waterman, and the black, wrought iron fence separating the Ivy League school from the rest of Providence arose on our left.

Also on the left was one of several icons we would pass that day: Carrie Tower. The clock tower stands at 95 feet of red brick with elaborate adornments. It was constructed by a husband in memory of his wife, Caroline Mathilde Brown, the granddaughter of the university's namesake. My favorite detail is the inscription in the foundation: Love is Strong as Death.

The view to the right was of a pair of libraries. The first building was the John Hay Library. From the outside, it is an impressive sight with massive wooden doors centered in a symmetrical arrangement of latticed windows. Hay used to be the primary library of the university, but it has evolved into the home for special collections, not the least of which was "the world's largest collection of American poetry and plays" according to Marla.

The next library on the right was the John D. Rockefeller, Jr. Library, which replaced Hay as the flagship library of Brown in 1964. To my unsophisticated eye, the new library lacks all of the charm of the older one, with a more modern style and dozens of tall, narrow windows.

In the discussion of the library, I discovered an aspect of Brown culture that I found especially endearing. The students at Brown (and would we call them Brownies?) employed a series of shortened names, pronounced acronyms, and nicknames to describe their world.

In this way, the John D. Rockefeller, Jr. Library became known to all as "the Rock."

But, according to legend, the donors who made the gift to build the library did not approve of the nickname. They demanded that students stop calling it "the Rock." It was only when students began to refer to it as "the John" that the donors acquiesced, said Marla with a smile.

These shortcut pronunciations abound at Brown. And the Rock is not the only library so affected. The Science Library was the site of the world's largest Tetris game in the year 2000. Students living in Technology House who shared a passion for technical projects – and apparently vintage video games – wired the outside of the monolithic 180-foot tall building and allowed fellow students to play the game in grand scale. The spelling of the Sciences Library has been shortened to "SciLi" and it is pronounced "sigh-lie."

Perhaps my favorite acronym to speak is the Program in Liberal Medical Education. The acronym is PLME, and it is pronounced "plee-me."

Another good example is the Verney-Wooley Dining Hall. An undergrad might be at a loss to direct you to this building, but ask about "V-Dub" and they'll get you there.

For what it is worth, V-Dub is an appetizing nickname for a dining hall when considered in context. The main competitor on campus for dining is the Sharpe Refractory, called "the Ratty." A fine name for a biology lab, I would think, but not a name that should spring to mind when one considers breakfast.

And, of course, Brown's immediate educational neighbor is the Rhode Island School of Design. This prestigious art school that regularly exchanges students back and forth with Brown is called "riz-dee."

Back to the tour, there was one more sight worth a mention here. The two libraries flank College Street, which descends steeply away from the campus. Across the road from the mouth of College Street are the Van Wickle Gates. The fence and wall that surround the oldest part of campus are broken in the center by a pair of black, wrought iron gates between two red brick pillars. Over the gates is the seal of the institution. The gates are opened only twice per year, and students typically only pass through the gates twice during their four-years at Brown: They march up College Street for Convocation at the beginning of their freshmen year, passing through the first time; the gates reopen at Commencement, and the graduates walk out the gates with their degrees.

As we walked, the mother of a prospective Brown undergraduate pointed to an academic building and asked our tour guide, Marla, "What is that building called?"

Marla scrunched up her face to think but couldn't come up with a name. She told us that this was her first day working as a tour guide since last year. Training was scheduled for next week, she said.

To my amusement, the tour became a tour of Marla's previous tours.

"I would usually take a tour into this quad," she mentioned at some point, gesturing to the right. She stopped walking and talking for a moment, and, coming to a decision, she turned us into the quad.

"We used to walk into the residence halls to examine a room," she said as we cruised by the buildings on Benevolent Street. But we didn't that day.

"I like to take tours into the building to look at a classroom," she confided as we stood in front of MacMillan Hall. We did not go in, but as the tour ended, she did say, "Oops! I wanted to take you into a classroom!"

We may have missed some pieces on the tour, but it was a great day for a walk through College Hill, and it helped to orient me to the campus.

*

Things were looking even better when I returned to the Admissions Office a few days later. The day that I took the tour, I noticed that the Admissions Office held information sessions each weekday. I had missed the session that day, so I decided to make a point of returning another time to catch the event.

I nodded to the ancient woman sitting behind the desk. She did not return the gesture, and I did not force the issue. I went into the same waiting area, which was now stuffed with parents and prospective students. I had modest expectations, but I sat down dutifully and waited.

A Brown student worker walked into the room and announced that the info session would begin momentarily. He pulled two chairs in front of the double doors leading to the foyer and took a seat in one of them.

And then in walked Scott.

I am comfortable enough in my heterosexuality to announce that Scott was painfully handsome. He looked like the actor Matthew McConaughey, with a smile that hinted at a vast world of private thoughts. He had wavy, longish hair, brown with blonde highlights. He wore nice blue slacks; a white button-down shirt, with no tie and the cuffs rolled a few turns; and brown moccasins with no socks.

As fun as Scott was to look at, he was also charming. He spoke with a subdued confidence and a gentle sense of humor. He explained that he had graduated Brown two years earlier after studying Egyptology, and he took a job in the Admissions Office over all of his other competing career opportunities.

He smiled at the prospective students and blushing mothers, and explained that he preferred to handle the session as an open-ended discussion. He questioned why people in the room were visiting Brown. He added that he hoped it was not because, geographically, Providence is on the route from New Haven to Cambridge.

52

Most of the kids in the room were reticent, so much so that a father put the first comment on the table: Brown is an Ivy League school. The potential students began opening up a bit. One said that she liked Brown's strong crew team. Another stated that the school had a reputation for rigorous classes but a laid-back student body. A third young audience member mentioned flexibility.

Scott asked the attendees how much they knew about Brown's flexibility. He went on to talk about the concentrations, the fact that a student can create a concentration, the lack of core requirements, and the ability to take courses as a pass/fail instead of a traditional letter grade. These flexible options are part of what is called the New Curriculum. To give a sense of the rate of change in academia, "New" in this case means adopted in the late 1960s. The bottom line is that the institution fosters an environment of self-directed study.

This point is at the core of the official culture of Brown. As I asked students questions throughout my time on campus – questions about the best classes, most popular concentrations, favorite activities, etc. – the most common answer was "It depends." That answer would make sense anywhere, but I heard it most often at Brown.

Brown is what each student makes of it. Undergraduates have a support system and network to pursue their interests. Each concentration has requirements and rigor built into it, but I met very few students who were not actively availing themselves of the freedom that Brown offered.

On this day, in this ornately decorated and lush room, with Scott talking to our group, I was not sure whether or not the message was getting through. Some parents were asking follow up questions about the flexibility of the New Curriculum, and I could hear skepticism in their voices. I even began to note some impatience. The prospective students were mostly silent.

53

Scott continued to smile and patiently answer questions until the group disbanded.

Brown is what each student makes of it, but as a result Brown is not for every student. And this fact is mutually recognized by applicants and the institution. I found many students at Brown who had applied to other Ivy League schools, but were only admitted to Brown. More interestingly, I found dozens of students at other Ivy League schools who were admitted to multiple Ivies, but denied at Brown. It supports my belief that Brown seeks a rare quality instead of – or in addition to – the qualities sought by its peers. As a result, there is a special cache in being admitted to Brown.

*

If the administration at Brown was not exactly warm and fuzzy in their reception of my project, I suppose I should not take it personally. I was in good company.

In early October, independent candidate for President of the United States, Ralph Nader, visited Brown University. Many aspects of the Nader visit were marred by controversy.

He was invited by a professor of English to speak, but according to Brown policy, any talk must be sponsored by a recognized university organization. The professor contacted political student groups on campus, but found no sponsors among them. Moreover, political candidates are barred from fundraising or campaigning on campus. A candidate may only give an informational or educational talk. Nader, however, said he would do both: Give an informational talk and actively campaign for votes. According to an article in the *Brown Daily Herald*, Nader himself stated that he was having a difficult time working with the Brown administration on his talk.

It was unclear at times whether or not the event would actually occur, but on a Wednesday afternoon,

Nader arrived in one of the biggest lecture halls on campus: Salomon 101.

I arrived early to see what kind of reception the students would give. I had spent some time with Libertarians at Brown, watching a presidential debate with them – a debate that excluded Nader. The Brown Green Party was an active group, and I bumped into their members around the campus. I had met both republican and democratic students. It was the democrats that I was most eager to see in the context of Nader's visit.

The feeling among democrats was that Nader was shanghaiing votes that would go to the democratic presidential candidate but for Nader's involvement. They blamed Nader for the loss of the then-previous presidential election by the democrats. Many students I met were passionate on this point. I heard plenty of nasty rhetoric about Nader and his visit. I was braced for a contentious day of protests.

My partner on this day was a student named Justin. Justin was an unusual Brown undergrad in several ways.

First, a learner in the Ivy League has the world open before him with a plethora of options from which to choose. Among all of the options open to Justin, he had his sights set on joining the Marine Corps following graduation. He was an athlete – of such quality that he missed part of the preceding academic year at Brown in a competitive effort to represent the United States in the Summer Olympics as a rower – and he wanted an equally tactile career. He also had a strong measure of patriotism, reflected in the fact that he was concentrating in American Studies.

Which brings us to the second factor that made Justin so unusual: Justin told me that he wasn't very smart. He went to Brown for the athletics, not the academics. That is another reason why he chose American Studies. According to him, it was one of the less rigorous concentrations.

The Things I Learned in College

Whether it was convincingly-delivered modesty, or whether Justin had the wisdom to recognize his own limitations, I found this news to be disarming and endearing.

Justin and I regularly went to the gym where he introduced me to coaches, staff members, and other athletes; and on this occasion, he agreed to come along to the political talk. As a republican, he did not have a big dog in the fight of the underwhelming independent candidate.

We stood in a line – thankfully, towards the front of the line – that wrapped around the building. We were contending for two of 500 available tickets. Democratic students passed out stickers to those of us waiting, each sticker announcing the names of their candidates. The conversation in the line was of the controversy of the visit, politics in general, and preliminary plans for spring break.

Once seated inside, the mood turned to nervous excitement. After an introduction by the English professor who instigated the visit, and multiple announcements about fire exits, Nader took the stage to warm, if not exuberant, applause. He seemed to have approximately eight enthusiastic supporters among the audience, and those supporters stood in the seats and clapped loudly while the other 492 of us looked on.

Nader's talk went over well with me. He began by saying that when he was of college age, he was at Princeton listening to similar talks. He criticized the two major party candidates for president. He expressed concern that the election was becoming more of a coronation with a foregone conclusion. He stated that his primary goal was to keep conversation going on topics that were important to him. He took pleasure in "getting people's dander up." His talk was marked by periods of applause, growing louder the more he spoke. He was moving the crowd – Justin and me along with everyone else – and I was impressed.

He asked the audience how many of them smoked marijuana. About a third of the crowd put up their hands. Another third of the audience seemed too stoned to respond.

When Nader finished speaking, he received a standing ovation from a large percentage of the audience – smokers and non-smokers alike.

Then came the questions and answers, where I heard what I expected from the students and a delightfully unexpected response from Mr. Nader.

Student's Comment: I understand what you are trying to do, but you have to see that it is counterproductive. You are taking votes away from the democratic candidate and helping the republicans to win the election. I hope at some point you look in the mirror and realize that you serve your country, and you drop out of the race.

Nader's Response: Would you ask the republican candidate, who is taking about 50 million votes from the democratic candidate, to drop out?

The student received both clapping and booing for his comment; Nader received hearty laughter and applause for his rejoinder.

I had plenty to consider as I walked away from the speech. Ralph Nader did a great job with the talk. The fact that he endured the difficulties of getting scheduled to speak on campus earned a bit more of my respect. I was equally impressed by the community at Brown that was capable of listening to the talk and being swayed – however mildly or temporarily. Those who were outspoken in their views were not always civil, but they were honest. I did not see much grandstanding or puffery. It was a day of honest exchanges and discussions.

*

I sat on the main green on a warm autumn day. I had just finished sitting in on a literature course where students were working through one of my favorite books, *The Time Traveler's Wife* by Audrey Niffenegger. I had a copy of the book and a couple of hours to kill before I was to join a lab class. The lab was part of a course taught by a Nobel Prize winning physicist, and I was assured a mind-blowing experience.

A great book, a beautiful day, and the promise of learning about superconductivity.

The view of the buildings from where I sat was inspiring. I was on the grass in front of Sayles Hall – appearing more like an impressive mansion than an academic building and leaking the sounds of a world-class music department – looking across at the back of University Hall. This symmetrical four-story building is the oldest building on campus, and it once provided shelter for George Washington and his troops in 1776. The building is flanked on the right by the white, Greek Revival-style Manning Hall, housing Manning Chapel and the Haffenreffer Museum of Anthropology; on the left squats the giant, red dormitory, Slater Hall.

The leaves were starting to flair with bright reds and oranges. The air smelled like New England in the fall. The open area of the main green was awash with students, sitting alone or in small groups, on the grass or on benches. Several Frisbee games were underway, and two men and a woman were tossing a football around in a triangle formation.

I was trying to enjoy the adventures taking place on the pages I was reading and trying to appreciate the exceptional environment . . . but I was driven to distraction by the fact that too many of the students around me had their butt cracks exposed.

It may have been the year's fashion trends that revealed so many unfortunate and unflattering body parts, but I sincerely doubt it. The reason why I don't believe this was the case is because so few of the people I could see were wearing anything that resembled modern fashion. The most memorable outfit of the day was a young lady wearing a pair of lime green and black plaid pants that appeared to be made out of felt and that – of course – drooped low enough to make any plumber blush. Memorable, but not unusual. Hemp-based clothing, shapeless hippie dresses, and corduroys were everywhere. I saw multiple women with buzz cuts or sporting dreadlocks.

It struck me often at Brown that the women seemed to rebel against traditional beauty trends. It wasn't that they were not attractive; it was that they seemed to be *trying* to appear physically unappealing.

The men, on the other hand, were a different story.

First, I had my encounter with Scott in the Admissions Office. At that time, I assumed that one beautiful man was a fluke. At least a man so attractive that I would notice.

Part of the oddity of my time at Brown is that it happened not once, but twice.

A friend of mine, Andrew, had attended Brown before I met him. When he heard about my project, he insisted that I meet up with the Brown Derbies. He said that they were an all-male a cappella group with which he used to sing.

To me, there were certain activities that I had never experienced, but which I regarded as quintessential of college life – especially at an Ivy. Fencing, fraternities, and *foie gras* all made the list. Another such activity was a cappella singing.

I had never experienced it firsthand, although I suppose if I had been asked, I might have had to search my memory to ensure that I really had not. I could describe it so readily that it seemed like I must have encountered it. A bunch of people singing with no instrumental accompaniment, performing different parts in unison, such that it produced a fuller sound.

I am confident, however, that I had not experienced collegiate a cappella prior to Brown. The reason I am confident is because I was so moved by it – so enthralled by it – that it is firmly etched into my memory. My prior thoughts on the topic were gray and two-dimensional. After Brown, they are rich and complex.

Andrew made an introduction for me, and I went to watch a dress rehearsal for the group in Wilson Hall. I walked in to find a group of about 15 young men dressed in khaki pants, white buttoned-up shirts, and non-matching ties. Each man wore a brown vest and either wore or fidgeted with a brown bowler hat.

Their conversations stopped when I tentatively stuck my head in the room. One of the members approached me, asking, "Are you Sean-Michael?" When I said yes, he smiled broadly and waved me into the room. "Derbies, this is Sean-Michael. He's writing a book about Brown. One of our distinguished alums sent him to us so he could see what we do. Cool?"

He began making the introductions. I met No-No, Cookie, Monkey, Nookie, Cherry, and the others in the group. Lots of handshaking and smiling and laughing. They were preparing for a big concert at the University of Connecticut that weekend. They started the year out by releasing an album with their renditions of some of my favorite songs on it. The collective group was ripe with charm, and I was smiling along with them.

Then came the singing. And it was good – better than I could have guessed or imagined. I recognized most songs as either classics or from the radio. Each person worked hard on their piece of the puzzle. The person singing lead, of course, was exerting effort, but even the guy making a "wah-wump" sound in the background was red faced with labor. The music – it wasn't singing exactly;

it was music – filled the room and my ears and my heart. They smiled and sang and smiled some more.

Somewhere along the way, I realized that the music was seductive. There was no overt romance to it – and I have a sexual aversion to both men and khakis – but listening to the Derbies was filling me with a euphoria that I associate with love.

That's how good it was: So good that I fell in love.

When the evening wrapped up, I thanked the Brown Derbies and walked away humming and doing a remarkably bad job of it.

*

One day, I sat down to write a bit of this chapter, and I began reading some of the more finished sections. I came across a sentence that read, "I saw several brown students sitting on the grass." The sentence bothered me, but it took me 20 seconds or so before I realized that the B in "brown" should have been capitalized.

I often raise eyebrows when I speak to my friends outside of Rhode Island about Brown University. I once told a friend, when I was excited about my visit to the school, "Brown rocks!"

"Where?" he asked, looking around.

Talking to my brother, Jason, I once mentioned, "Brown is fun."

Very seriously, he responded, "I prefer blue."

Perhaps the best example was a conversation that I had with my grandmother. She asked me what I was learning on my trip. I replied, "Well, most Brown students are as smart as the students that I met elsewhere.

She leaned forward and patted my hand. "Good for you," she said with a smile.

*

Katie is one of my very best friends. We met in law school at Cornell, where she was one year behind me. We worked in the Legal Aid Clinic together, and we had mutual friends. We worked within two desks of each other for a couple of months before we had our first conversation, but as soon as we started talking, we never stopped. She comforted me when my mother died and I comforted her when her father died. We forged a close and enduring bond.

And, as luck would have it, she earned her undergraduate degree at Brown.

I told Katie that she should visit me at some point during my stay at the university. She had just moved to New York City and started her new job at one of the most prestigious law firms on Wall Street. She was not exactly lonely – more than half of her class at law school moved to New York with her – but she agreed that it would be a treat to steal away for a weekend. Besides, she had not visited the school in the five years since her graduation, and she thought it would be nice to reminisce.

Thus, on a Friday after work, she caught a train and came to Providence, Rhode Island. She hopped off the train, dressed in a smart attorney costume, and bounded into my car. "There is so much that we need to see!" she exclaimed without preamble, directing me towards the Federal Hill neighborhood of Providence.

"Oh, I missed this place!" Katie exclaimed as we pulled up to an Italian restaurant.

I was a bit turned around, so I asked her, "Where are we in relation to Brown?"

"The same city, but that's about it as far as relation," she responded. I had imagined that we would stroll through her memories of campus, but the allure of pasta was more than she could bear.

As we went in, Katie whispered to me, "Be cool. This place is run by the mafia."

I glanced around and tried to be cool.

Over a dinner of clams and noodles and shrimp and veal, Katie brought me up to date on her adventures. Katie was beginning her law career, hobnobbing with our old classmates, and pursuing love. A beautiful and tough lesbian, she was struggling to find a partner – a struggle that took us through several courses of our meal.

She asked me about my project, and I assured her that she would get to see it in action the next day.

We spent the night at the Hope Club – Katie being a member of the Cornell Club which had a reciprocity agreement with the club at Brown – and awoke the next day fresh and ready.

And apparently hungry.

This was a day of eating. We went to La Creperie for breakfast and had some of the best crepes I had ever had – including crepes I had in Paris over two periods of studying at the Sorbonne. We went to Wings to Go and ate more wings than would be decent to quantify. We went to Paragon, Kartabar, *and* Andreas for dinner. And, of course, we went to the Ratty and the GBC – that is, the Grad Center Bar – during the day.

These bouts of decadent feasting were wedged between seeing the sights. To our credit, we ran twice that day for a total of approximately seven miles.

The first and longer run was to get the lay of the land. We left the Hope Club and ran past WBRU – a fully functioning commercial radio station run by Brown students. The station is no typical student station. It was honored by *Rolling Stone* magazine as a medium range radio station a number of times. During her undergraduate days, Katie hosted a segment from 2 to 5 a.m. under the handle "Lady Katie" – a play on words with the time of her shift and her gender – until she was promoted to the Retro Lunch Show.

We ran down the hill and through the neighborhoods before running up College Street as she recounted her experiences passing through the Van

Wickle Gates. We ran over to Thayer Street, and Katie pointed to the mouth of a tunnel for buses that runs under the campus to the bottom of College Hill. She told me a story about John F. Kennedy, Jr. rolling a bowling ball down the two-lane tube when he was an undergraduate at Brown. The story is not true, unfortunately – an urban legend attributed to several noteworthy alumni.

We headed to Pembroke – the original women's college. Brown started admitting female students in 1891 and started serving them more fully, but decidedly segregatedly in 1903 through Pembroke College. Although the final vestiges of this segregation were removed in 1971 with the official merger, Pembroke remains a distinguishable entity at Brown. Katie lived in dormitories in Pembroke, and we spent some time running around and through the buildings. She carefully leapt over the Pembroke seal at Alumnae Hall due to the generally-held superstition that a woman would become pregnant if she stepped on it. A long shot, in Katie's case, I would think.

The second run, attempted on a belly full of wings, was from the Hope Club up to and through the athletic complex northwest of campus. As we ran, I told Katie about my friend Justin. We were invited to meet Justin at a fraternity party that night. The theme was the 1980s. While we did not have much in the way of costumes, our contributions could be actual memories of the 1980s.

Katie and I arrived at the fraternity house behind the Ratty around 10 p.m. The house and its courtyard were occupied – but not packed – with students sporting the worst fashions of the 80s: the women with big hair, plastic jewelry, tube tops, and stretchy pants; the men all looking either like Don Johnson or Malcolm-Jamal Warner. Culture Club, a-ha, and Michael Jackson tunes ripped through the night.

Within minutes of our arrival, my friend Justin walked out of a back room with a few friends. He was holding a plastic cup containing an adult beverage – certainly not his first, second, or fifth of the night – and he sloshed a bit of it out as he gave me a giant hug.

"This is the writer dude!" he yelled to his friends. Focusing on Katie, Justin said, "You must be his girlfriend."

"No," Katie responded. "I'm just a friend."

In retrospect, Justin's initial tone with Katie could be best described as respectful. Once the word "friend" passed from Katie's lips, Justin had switched to seduction mode. "What's a pretty girl like you doing in a place like this?" A long and heavy arm slipped around her shoulders.

"Whoa, big fella!" Katie said, starting to twist and turn.

Justin leaned close. "What do you say we get out of here?"

"Okay, you first."

"Come on, baby," he whispered. I could almost see Justin's breath, but I could definitely see Katie's reaction to it.

"Okay, that's it!" Katie declared to me. "I'm playing the L card!" Looking up at Justin, she stated, "I'm a lesbian."

He looked confused. He dangled the question, "So then you're...?"

"Gay. All kinds of gay. Very, very gay." He still seemed confused, partially by Katie and partially by the rancorous laughter of his friends. To be helpful, Katie said, "I like girls."

Justin smiled broadly and gave her a squeeze. "I do, too!" he exclaimed. He pulled her deeper into the party, saying, "Come on, let's go find some!"

I caught one last look at a wide-eyed Katie disappearing around a corner.

Katie and Justin returned about 20 minutes later, the best of friends and in cahoots on their mission. "There are no girls here," said Justin, and Katie nodded in support.

I gestured vaguely at the room full of co-eds.

"No, not these girls," responded Katie. "We need *real* girls. These ones are too clean and fluffy." This time Justin nodded with enthusiasm.

"What do you want? Strippers?" I asked sarcastically.

Suddenly, I had four unblinking eyes focused on me.

"No," I said slowly. "You don't want that."

"Hell yes we do!" said Justin.

"Come on," said Katie. "Take us to a strip club!"

"Yeah, come on. Please?"

Despite my trepidation, I did see a relevant tangent that could take us there. I had read a book called, *Ivy League Stripper* by Heidi Mattson, an alumna of Brown University who stripped to pay her way through college. The book was a great read, fresh in my mind, and centered on the university I was researching.

I caved and agreed to take them to a strip club. Thirty days at each of the eight schools, and I am sure that at no point had I ever made two people happier.

Justin rounded up a couple of friends and we left the party in search of nipples.

We crammed into my car, with Katie in the passenger seat and Justin and several athletes stuffed into the back. Justin was eager to share the experience with his peers at Brown, and he was working his cell phone.

Talking to one of his friends on the phone, he took a tone that was half heckling and half pleading. "Come on! You can do it. Just meet us there. No, you're going! Come on! You fag!"

The color immediately drained from his face as he looked to Katie. He muttered, "Sorry," in such a forlorn voice that Katie laughed uncontrollably for the better part of the night.

As we drove, I became aware that not one of my passengers – Katie included – had ever visited a strip club. They had questions ranging from etiquette to the degree of nudity we would encounter.

We found the club. We went in. We learned.

Perhaps it was my age or perhaps it was prior experience – I was a Marine, after all – but I emerged from the adventure unscathed. My friends, however, left considerably poorer, but in very good spirits. Several of them had fallen in love that night, and those who did were confident that their love was returned. Katie talked of a return visit to go on a date with Bambi, a young woman who said that she was trying to earn enough money to put her elderly grandmother in a better nursing facility.

Education and intelligence are no match for nudity and love.

*

Brown was an interesting experience. Because I had so little prior experience with the institution, I imagine I relied a bit more heavily on the stereotypes that I had heard.

My visit did little to dispel some of the stereotypes. The students who were drawn to Brown and the students that Brown selected manifested a different-thinking ethic. It could often be seen in their projects, clubs, classes, and clothing. They were not produced like cookies on an assembly line. In some ways, they reminded me of concoctions formed from the stuff between the punched out cookies – different and odd, but just as tasty and twice as interesting.

One stereotype that took a beating from my vantage point was the reputation as a liberal school. I suppose there are multiple ways to view liberalness. Pot smoking?

Sure. Plenty of opposing viewpoints? Yep. But tolerant and welcoming? I didn't see as much of that. I saw different factions, but I didn't see the Pollyanna co-mingling of factions that I associate with liberalness.

One of the best things that happened during my time at Brown University is that I discovered that I was on to something. I suppose I had some initial concern that my project would reveal that the Ivies were identical, and that I would spend eight months living the same experience over and over again. I was only two schools deep into my journey, but my experience at Brown was not the same as my experience at Cornell. On the one hand, this was an incredible relief; on the other, it made me more aware that I could not predict what awaited me at Dartmouth and beyond.

DARTMOUTH COLLEGE

Q: How many Dartmouth students does it take to screw in a light bulb?

A: None – Hanover doesn't have electricity.

The official motto of Dartmouth College is "A voice crying in the wilderness," which, as I like to translate it, could be, "Help! I'm lost in the woods!" When it comes to school mottos, it doesn't get much better than that.

Going into this project, Dartmouth was one of my favorite schools. I had never attended, but I had visited once when I considered attending the Tuck School of Business. Every Ivy had special appeal for me, but I had Dartmouth upon a precarious pedestal.

I rolled into the small and quaint town of Hanover in mid-October ready to explore and learn.

*

The problem, as I recognized when I arrived in Hanover, New Hampshire, was that it was completely foreign to me.

Cornell was practically home. I had plenty of friends and years of memories and experiences on which to draw. Brown was a new environment to me, but I had Katie and the comforts of Providence to welcome me.

I had not spent much time at Dartmouth previously. I did not know anyone there. Beyond these basic observations, getting assimilated into the community presented new challenges. Dartmouth was the first and only school in my travels that completely dominated its surroundings. At Brown, I could hover on Thayer Street with its dozens of restaurants, bars, and shops; and I could interact with students and experience some of the culture of the institution.

At Dartmouth, there is no Thayer Street. There are East Wheelock and North Main Streets, with a handful of stores and restaurants set up to serve those who are a part of the Dartmouth community. I felt conspicuous. Every school had insiders and outsiders, but in this case, the town itself had insiders and outsiders.

A practical problem that came with the foreignness of Hanover was where I would live for my 30 days and nights. The Hanover Inn seemed to be a great choice – located directly across from the green and offering inspired views of Dartmouth – but the cost was prohibitive for a long-term stay. I began to envision a camping adventure in the deep woods.

The path I chose was much closer to camping than to a four-star hotel.

The Dartmouth, the student newspaper, published a story about my project. Within a couple of hours, I received an e-mail from a student asking me if I would like to stay with a group of Dartmouth undergrads living off campus. Setting aside the fact that I was homeless in October in New Hampshire, the opportunity to live with a group of undergrads was one that I could not refuse.

I responded, and he invited me to come to his place to meet his roommates. He called the house "the Experiment." He gave me directions that took me down the hill from Dartmouth and across the river into the State of Vermont. I missed the turn off of the side street a couple of times before I realized that I was looking for a dirt trail, dropping impossibly off of the blacktop and sending my car through the trees. A twist or two, and I came upon the house.

The Experiment sat by itself in a clearing in the woods, large and sprawling, looking more unfinished than broken. Exposed insulation, a patchwork of wooden and plastic siding, and a mish-mash of doors decorated the structure. The yard had multiple fire pits and seating areas.

Inside, the house was even more schizophrenic. The furniture was battered and mismatched. There were blankets and curtains hanging, sometimes on windows, sometimes on walls, and sometimes blocking off living areas. I discovered that the house had three stories and at least a dozen bedrooms – or spaces used as bedrooms. The kitchens and bathrooms . . . well, this was a place where only 20-year-old men lived, and they lived as only 20-year-old men can.

On that first day, I met with five Dartmouth students living in the house. I lived with them for 30 days, but I never saw some of those people again. People may have moved in and out, or they may have spent nights elsewhere, but the academic, athletic, and social schedules of a student at Dartmouth can be demanding.

More strikingly, I was never able to figure out how many people lived in the Experiment with me. I asked many people many times, but I never had an accurate count. In fact, one morning over a bowl of Frosted Flakes, I encountered a smartly dressed young man who stated that he lived on the third floor. We shook hands and introduced ourselves for the first time after living together for nearly a month.

*

Alcohol was a touchy subject at Dartmouth during the time of my visit. I can make two generalizations based on my observations and conversations at the school:

1. Liquor was more central to life at Dartmouth than at any other Ivy.
2. The state, town, and college worked harder to curb illegal alcohol consumption compared with the environment at other Ivies.

71

Set aside for a minute how influential Greek life is at Dartmouth, with more than half of the undergraduate student body participating in approximately 30 Greek organizations. Set aside that the hit movie *National Lampoon's Animal House* was inspired by the writer's experiences as a fraternity brother at Dartmouth. You are still left with a story involving plenty of booze.

The easy answer – and possibly the true answer – is to point at the surrounding landscape and wonder what alternative activities are available. But alcohol seems to run deeper than boredom – especially in an age where people have so many options.

As with any generalization, there are notable exceptions. I ate Indian food with a group of teetotalers, and I met people at every turn – including in the Greek system – who did not drink. But even those who did not partake did comment. Drinking was the culture; not drinking was the counterculture; and people seemed to be aware of this state of affairs.

The more interesting story was the enforcement of drinking restrictions and ordinances. Most of the students with whom I discussed drinking had strong and negative opinions on the topic of the enforcement. They felt persecuted, perhaps unfairly, and they were angry.

Students who were caught drinking underage or publically could find themselves in trouble of various sorts. School-trouble was one thing, but it was trouble from outside the Dartmouth community that was most feared. Hefty fines and permanent arrest records were among the concerns that plagued the students. A zero tolerance policy may or may not have curtailed some measure of drinking, but it appeared to me that some of the drinking was almost in spite of the strict enforcement.

The spite seemed to be caused in part by the tactics employed by those who would enforce the rules. The enforcement officials would allegedly wear plain clothes and sit in anticipation in local liquor stores, waiting to make a bust. Town and state enforcement officers would walk through the college grounds – turf that the undergraduates felt was theirs by achievement and by tuition dollars. Moreover, these non-uniformed enforcement officials would infiltrate parties looking for abuses.

I appreciated both sides of the argument. The tactics did not seem overly heavy-handed to me. The people who usually suffered under these tactics were those who were breaking the law. On the other hand, it created a climate of fear that infected the non-guilty alongside the guilty. It drew attention to a problem, but the attention did not seem to be either effective or healthy.

And it certainly slowed me down. My presence at parties across the northeast was often met with some apprehension, but Dartmouth students often had to be reassured that I was not interested in seeing their age-designating bracelets, examining their IDs, or smelling their breath. Particularly this last piece.

*

Every Ivy, Dartmouth included, has traditions and activities. Some activities serve niche groups, some are not officially sanctioned by the institution, and some are traditions passed down from one class to another. It would be difficult to count the number of activities that each student views as central to the culture of the school.

At Dartmouth, however, many students agreed that there were four major events representing the four seasons of the year.

By most accounts, Green Key Weekend was the most obscure of the seasonal events. Taking place in the spring, the event is a long weekend of parties and activities on campus. My impression is that the significance of the event is to serve as an activity for spring so that Dartmouthers can claim an event in each season.

The Winter Carnival, on the other hand, is a major event with a clear theme. The theme changes each year and ranges from the Great Cold Rush to Camelot Frozen in Time to the Roaring 20 Degrees. The themes often relate to the year – for example, after the turn of the millennium, they celebrated 2001: An Ice Odyssey – or to pop culture, such as the One Carnival to Rule them All, to coincide with the release of the final chapter of the *Lord of the Rings* movies in theaters.

The theme during the year that I visited was Oh, The Places It Snows: A Seussentennial. The event celebrated the birthday of one of Dartmouth's most famous alumni: Theodor Geisel, otherwise known as Dr. Seuss. He graduated in 1925, a true Dartmouth man: Not only did he go on to pursue a doctorate in literature at Oxford University before earning fame and fortune, but he joined a fraternity at Dartmouth and was once penalized for getting caught drinking alcohol.

Alas, I arrived the fall following the February event, and I was gone before the next one arrived.

I also missed the event that I imagine would have been my favorite had I been so fortunate as to be a Dartmouth student: Tubestock. This summer event occurred on the Connecticut River, walking distance from the campus. Students would bring their inner tubes, rafts, and other floatation devices and have a party while floating on the river. (Years after my time at Dartmouth, this event was officially banned and outlawed – almost certainly a smart move, but one that makes me feel like a door has been permanently closed to me.)

My event was one that occurs on all Ivy League campuses: Homecoming. I'm certain that each school has homecoming traditions worthy of this book, but let me tell you what I witnessed at Dartmouth.

It all began with a wooden pyre in the middle of the green. It is challenging to appreciate how *visible* this spot is unless you have passed through Hanover at some point. In an area of so many trees, the absence of trees is usually marked by a building or structure of some sort. The green is conspicuous for its openness. Standing on East Wheelock Street and looking towards the campus, one can survey the five-acre green ringed with trees – which, by the time of Homecoming are more or less bare of leaves – and crossed by a network of foot paths. And standing in the center of this open space was a wooden edifice several stories tall.

I walked by the flammable structure in the late afternoon of Friday, October 29, on my way to have dinner with a group of students at an apartment on Allen Street. The structure of the pyre was fully built, with the number of the freshmen class year prominently displayed in wood at the top. Security was posted around its base. Spectators – mostly alumni, families, and members of the Hanover community – were setting up chairs and choosing their spots.

At my dinner, I queried the assembled classmates about the rest of Homecoming.

"Is anyone going to the game tomorrow?" Dartmouth was playing Harvard in football on Saturday morning, and Homecoming is a football tradition.

A couple of people were debating going to see the women's hockey game in the afternoon, but no one seemed especially interested in the football game. (The game, as it turned out, was close, but Dartmouth lost.)

"So what else will you do this weekend?" I wondered.

Not surprisingly, many in the group of a dozen or so seniors referenced studying or writing papers. They mentioned that they would miss the parade, but they had seen it multiple times before, and they were happy enough to skip it this year.

I would be remiss if I did not at least mention one specific member of the dinner party. With a gargantuan red beard, brown work boots, and beige-colored overalls over a red flannel shirt, he looked like he was entering a lumberjack contest. He seemed cranky – and goodness knows, he probably had a hatchet on him somewhere – so we didn't interact much, but it tickled me to meet a student who looked the way Dartmouth felt to me.

The next time I saw the wooden structure on the green, it was moments away from the lighting. The freshmen arrived on the scene at 8 p.m. led by a bagpiper. It was a perfect, clear night, with the full moon high above Dartmouth Hall.

When lit, the structure went up in a rush of smoke. The flames reached impossibly high. The crowd was massive, and the celebration was palpable. As I pushed through the singing and dancing crowd, I could feel the heat of the fire and I could observe the annual ritual in full swing.

Running around the base of the inferno were more than 1,000 freshmen. Tradition held that the freshmen class would circle the bonfire one time for each year representing their year of graduation. Thus, the class of 1999 ran around the fire 99 times. At the turn of the millennium, the students had a choice to make, but – human nature being what it is – no one wanted to see the next class have it easier than the class before it, so the class of 2000 ran around the fire 100 times.

To be sure, running more than 100 revolutions around this structure is no small feat. It is big, and the distance is enough to wind an athlete; but it isn't that big, and dizziness becomes an issue. The heat is also a hindrance. The temperature that night dipped below freezing, but many of the more prepared runners were dressed in shorts and many men were running topless.

And then there were the rugby players.

My housemates at the Experiment – by and large – played rugby for Dartmouth, and they advised me in advance about one of the team's traditions. If the class ran clockwise around the bonfire, the freshmen rugby players ran counterclockwise. Just another complication in an already challenging event.

I stood cheering on the class in the flickering light of the bonfire. When the class year atop the structure collapsed, I booed along with the crowd. For me – with a great deal of affection for Dartmouth, but no formal affiliation with the school – the night was both memorable and meaningful.

And not because it was the second-closest I came to catching on fire during my 30 days at the school.

*

My housemates in the Experiment warned me about my room, saying that it gets pretty cold at night.

They were right.

Upon closer inspection, my room was more of a porch than a room. It had a ceiling and a couple of walls, but the remainder of the enclosure was porous and flimsy. By early November, I was sleeping on my air mattress in a sweat suit wearing multiple pairs of socks with as many blankets as I could find. I would wake some mornings slightly surprised to be alive, with my water bottle frozen solid inches from my head.

The room came with a kerosene heater of some sort. I'm sure that it was not approved for indoor use, but I am not sure that I was technically indoors, and I was grateful for the heat.

Strange smells were not uncommon in the Experiment. In fact, I assume that the name "the Experiment" was assigned on an olfactory basis. Without opening the refrigerator or stepping into the bathroom, the house smelled of spaghetti sauce, marijuana, and sweat. It wasn't unpleasant, but it was a defining feature of life there.

Early one morning, however, I woke to a new smell. I struggled to wake up, and I found that I was slightly on fire. I had curled around the heater in my sleep, and my sweatshirt and pants were actively smoldering. Thick, dark smoke was arising from holes burned through my clothes – black encircled with orange embers.

I patted out the embers with the mittens I was wearing, slid a few inches away from the heater, and returned to my dream of spooning with the sun.

*

Fraternities are private affairs. I was mindful of how special and rare it was every time I was welcomed into a meeting with a fraternity. Even at a party, I was aware that I was an outsider being given an exceptional honor. To be embraced by any community is a treat, but to be embraced by one that is defined by the fact that it is selective in whom it counts as a member is even better.

I spent some time with fraternities at Dartmouth. Great guys to whom I am appreciative. But I am sure that they would understand if I quickly moved past writing about my adventures there to get to the rarer and weirder experience that I had when I was adopted by a sorority at Dartmouth.

It began with Claire who invited me to watch the fencing team practice. That led to an invitation to a Halloween party in the sorority house. I intended to dress up as a guy conducting research for a book, although I suppose I did a better job of pulling off creepy-old-guy. The women and their guests, however, were gracious and kind. They attempted to teach me their version of beer pong – every group seems to have a twist on the game; one that is always lost on me and one about which they are extremely proud – and they talked with me about life at the school. The women were funny and smart, and I was grateful for the experience.

Thus, you can imagine my delight when they invited me to attend a closed meeting of their private group. I readily accepted, of course, and only then began to wonder what I would see. I was pretty sure – although not entirely certain – that women left to their own devices do not spontaneously engage in pajama-clad pillow fights, but I could not imagine what I would find.

I arrived to find 30 young women gathering in the common room of their house in the middle of campus – dressed comfortably, but not in pajamas. The meeting assembled with Claire sitting on one side of me and Amy, a noteworthy beer pong champion, on the other side. Claire was the officer of the week and charged with facilitating the meeting.

The ladies began by flinging about "thank yous." Some were generally cast – "Thank you for registering to vote" – and some were specific – "Thank you for fixing my pantyhose." While they thanked each other, they threw candy at each other playfully and fed each other green Jell-O shots. At one point, a sister shouted out, "Whose bra is this?" and held up a silky black undergarment. The non sequitur got many laughs, and the garment was ultimately reclaimed by its owner. The atmosphere was full of comradery and friskiness. Perhaps a pillow fight was not out of the question.

As the agenda progressed to logistics, the sisters began to discuss a scholarship meeting with the deans of the college, maintenance issues with the house, and an upcoming party. On this last issue, Claire said, "We are thinking this will be a more chill atmosphere, not as much beer as wine for those who want to *drink...*"

Claire was cut off when, beside me, Amy leapt to her feet. She did it with a suddenness and dexterity that shocked me. Even stranger, four other girls jumped up at the same time. One girl, upon standing, took a deep theatrical bow. Another did jumping jacks beside one who seemed to be imitating a cheerleader. Amy yelled something. In my surprise, I must have misheard what she said. What are the odds that she actually belted out, "I'm a tomato!"?

The girls sat back down just as quickly, surrounded by laughter. Looking around, I discovered that the laughs were provoked more by my reaction than the actions of the girls. "Those are our pledges," stated Claire. "They have rules and when they hear certain words in these meetings, it triggers them."

I looked at Amy. "I'm a pledge," she confirmed.

"And, apparently, a tomato," I said. She nodded proudly while the girls broke into more laughter.

"Maybe this is a good time for pledge entertainment," Claire suggested.

The five pledges stood in the middle of the circle of young women sitting on the floor. Someone started the music, and the pledges began a choreographed dance number. Well, perhaps choreographed is too generous. It was the dancing equivalent of several patients suffering seizures simultaneously. I tried to watch, but I just couldn't.

The dance ended as punch bowls were brought out. One was alcoholic and the other was non-alcoholic, and the girls assembled into two teams with straws. The game was to drink it all as fast as possible. I was invited to join the virgin group, and I gave it my best, but we were soundly beaten. In fairness, we had three pledges against their two who had to stop and go through their routines when the word "drink" was spoken.

One game led into another. They played Mad Libs where pretty much every noun was a penis and every verb was a sexual act. When the game called for the name of a person in the room, someone shouted out, "Let the boy be the person!" And so I was.

A pledge did a belly dance. She was actually really good and I was easily able to watch – until I became aware that the girls were watching me watch. And when they saw me watching them watching me watch her – and when they saw the shade of red that I turned – they erupted in laughter at me and applause for her.

A quick round of charades followed. "Make the boy do it!" and I did my best impression of a spaceship.

A rousing rendition of Happy Birthday by the whole house directed at Claire.

The games and singing eventually turned to talking. One sister had a new baby cousin. A picture was circulated to the sound of many "awwwhhhhs" and "so cutes" atop the thumping of many young biological clocks. There was talk of other Greek organizations. The ladies volunteered their observations about different societies and shared stories of some of their interactions with members of fraternities. One girl told a story about her boyfriend. "He is a political conservative in general, but he is undecided. He sent me a Blitz" – a Dartmouth-only form of electronic mail that predates actual e-mail, and a system that students still favored over actual e-mail at the time of my visit – "that said that I was more important to him than politics, so he would vote democrat in the election." The girls made appreciative noises. She ended her story with, "Plus, I told him that I wouldn't have sex with him anymore if he didn't."

These are some of my observations at the meeting. I witnessed funny and touching moments, and I was exposed to a few secrets that I need to keep to myself. I left dizzy with embarrassment and respectful of the privilege. So powerful was the experience that it was hours before I realized – with only slight disappointment – that if there was a pillow fight, it happened after I left.

*

I sat in on several courses at Dartmouth, but there was one professor who was recommended almost universally in the psychology department, and her classes were among my favorites during the course of the entire project. I sat in on her Adolescence course multiple times, and I always walked away thinking.

In one class, the students participated in an interesting exercise. The professor stuck a post-it note on each class member's forehead. The notes had numbers on them, and the students could not see their own numbers. The participants were then charged with pairing up with others – without talking – to get the highest combined score. Thus, each student was encouraged to find and pair with partners with the highest numbers.

The activity was interesting as a simulation for human pairing. Some students competed against each other to win the attention of those with the highest numbers. Participants with multiple suitors picked the one with the highest score, but at least one suitor tried to isolate a partner with a high number, attempting to hide the number from classmates. In many cases, couples would form, only to be broken when a higher number came along. In the end, high number couples emerged, along with many couples who had to settle for a number close to their own.

This exercise led to an hour of excited debriefing and learning about the way that romantic partnerships form. And the value of a realistic assessment of one's own number.

But even the Adolescence classes that did not involve such dramatic activities were full of interesting and entertaining lectures and discussions.

"Let's go back to where we left off last time," said the prof at the beginning of a class. "We were talking about physiological acts that correspond with psychological phenomena. For instance, who can tell me what is involved in smiling?"

The class members offered various bits: We smile when we are happy or trying to appear happy; we smile when we are attempting to connect with other humans; and the act of smiling involves the use of many facial muscles.

The professor asked, "Are humans the only animals that smile?"

This was debated at length. A contingent of students insisted that their family dogs could, and would, smile. The professor probed, "What does it mean when a dog smiles at you?" A long silence. "A baring of the teeth is a sign of extreme aggression. Fido doesn't love you – he wants to eat you!

"So what does this mean about the human smile?" She pointed out the seemingly paradoxical nature of a human smile. Our eyes are soft and welcoming, but our mouths are clearly engaged in an act that indicates aggression in nature.

"Okay," the professor said. "Let's move beyond physiological actions and talk about development. Who can give me an example of physiological development that correlates with psychological behavior?" A few hands shot up. "Yes, Jeff?"

One of the four men in the 25-person class ventured, "Ah, nipples?"

Over a few snickers, the professor asked, "What about nipples?"

"Ah, we like having them touched?"

"Okay," the professor said, addressing the class. "We aren't just gaining insight into Jeff here. Let's stick with this: What happens when we have our nipples fondled?"

"Our brains release oxytocin," stated a girl in the middle of the semi-circular tiered room.

"Right! A powerful neurotransmitter is released, and it feels like pleasure or love in your body. So what is the physiological development piece of this?" Silence. "Do people with more oxytocin develop bigger nipples?" Some shuffling, and then the professor admitted, "I have no idea. Jeff – you should look into this for us." I saw him make a note, and I had the distinct impression that he was going to research this question.

The conversation eventually moved to an example that I find interesting: Apparently the hormone that causes women to develop large, pointy chins is also associated with aggressive behavior. A psychological and biological explanation for the popular depiction of witches.

But the discussion also evolved in entertaining and thought-provoking directions, including a tangent on the word "penis" – starting with how funny of a word it is and ending with how funny looking the actual objects are to those who do not encounter them every day.

This particular professor was not only an entertaining and insightful teacher. She managed an active research agenda examining the brains of teenagers. She ran a lab equipped with an MRI machine, and she was collecting data to determine – among other things – at what age the human brain fully developed.

One of the students who convinced me to meet the professor was Helen. Helen knew the professor from class and from the lab where Helen worked as an undergraduate research assistant under the professor. But in the small community of Dartmouth, an over-achieving and student-centric professor does more than research and teaching. In this case, the professor served as an advisor to the sorority of which Helen was elected president.

To me, both of these women were the epitome of the Ivy League: Hard working, ambitious, and dedicated to service.

Helen helped me more than once during my project. Introducing me to the psychology professor was certainly her biggest contribution, but a close second involved election night.

84

Higher education inspires a great deal of political debate. Students explore different points of view. Some develop an inordinate devotion to one cause or another. Sometimes those devotions are tenacious and sometimes they are fickle, but they are often full of passion.

I was fortunate enough to conduct my project during the year of a presidential election. Thus, I was able to see the rallies and the campaigning on all sides of major debate.

It just so happened that I was geographically close to one side of the debate. One of my housemates, Steve, was the president of the Dartmouth College Democrats – the largest of the partisan political groups on campus. He worked tirelessly across the campus, the community, and the region in support of his candidate. He was one of the most impressive students I met on campus based in part on his intellect and passion for politics, based in part on his athletic ability as a member of the men's rugby team, and based in part on his willingness to occasionally wash dishes in the Experiment.

The campus had plenty of republicans, and a contingent of extremely outspoken libertarians, but with an excess of democrats on hand and their leader sleeping two rooms away, I was over-exposed to the democrats' messages. Moreover, the organization of the collegiate democrats dramatically outpaced the republicans. Democratic rally-goers and sign-carriers abounded in loud and smiling masses – waving, chanting, and proselytizing – day in and day out leading up to the election. I only saw a small collection of sign waving republican supporters on one occasion. They were not smiling or enthusiastic, and when I questioned them, I discovered that they were neither Dartmouth students nor volunteers. They were paid to wave their signs until 5 p.m., and at 5:01 they disbanded with no trace that they had ever been there. My world was overrun with formidable democrats, and the election result seemed to be a foregone conclusion.

When Helen asked me to join her sorority to watch the election returns, I went in with full confidence that the rest of the country was in lock step with the political climate in Hanover, New Hampshire. After leaving a politically diverse – but still democratic-heavy – group of students watching the early returns in the Collis Center, I joined both Helen and Steve in a sorority house on Webster Avenue watching history happen.

At 9:40 p.m., the republicans were ahead 170 electoral votes to the democrats' 112. The democratic crowd with which I sat booed and hissed, occasionally shouting "Fuck you!" at the television when republican returns came in or issuing a loud cheer when a state went for their party. While we watched, some of the spectators played drinking games. One girl sat on the floor with a large scale knitting project on her lap. Some undergrads argued politics, including Steve. One pretty girl in her early 20s commented inexplicably every time commentator James Carville appeared on the television, with pearls such as, "He's so hot!" and "I would have his babies in a second!"

At the risk of springing a spoiler on you, my dear reader, the republicans took the presidential election that year. I was shocked. I left after midnight, the writing clearly on the wall, in a haze of disbelief.

Part of what I learned that night was about the relative isolation of life at a top-tier school. Not to oversimplify a complicated matter, but it is possible to forget that life at a university is unusual. The people are smart and passionate and affluent and opinionated and impressionable and fortunate and young. It is a big world filled with lots of people, and an Ivy League community is not often a reliable representative sample.

The experience of watching the students react throughout the night to the returns was significant for me. The students were passionate, evidenced by the insults, cheers, and pizza being hurled at the television. Steve, however, was graceful and subdued. All of his effort did not amount to the big win, but he took it in stride. I saw him the next day, in a class, smiling and furiously taking notes. That night in the Experiment, he confided that he was glad the election was over. His ultimate goal was to write, and he hoped to have more time to devote to that activity now. He was resilient, and I was impressed by him.

That is one of the bits of magic floating through the Ivy League. The classes and dorms and organizations are full of winners. They come in as winners, and many go on to win even bigger. The setbacks they face in the relative safety of their schools can help them to develop the skills and disposition they need to win the next time, or to lose with a grace that is uncommon among the masses.

I'm confident that wherever Helen and Steve go, they will be stronger for their time at Dartmouth; and I am a little bit stronger for having met them.

*

One random school day, with the smell of late fall in the air, I set out across campus on an adventure.

I parked off of Maynard Street, deep on the campus. I popped into the red brick structure of Moore Hall, waving to a few psychology students on my way through and peeking in the lab to see my overachieving and hilarious professor.

Cutting back outside, I passed Kemeny Hall and the Haldeman Center to slip into the back of Carson Hall. Up a flight of steps and through a long corridor, passing the open Mac computers where I would often stop to check my e-mail, and into the Baker Library. Instead of continuing into the stacks and study spaces of Baker, I left through the front door.

If someone set out at that moment to take a non-aerial picture of Dartmouth – something iconic – they would have captured me in that picture. The green spread out before me, and I could see the Hanover Inn on the other side of East Wheelock Street. I stood under the Baker bell tower with its clock and weather vane.

Flanking the left side of the green sat another Dartmouth landmark: Dartmouth Hall. This structure of white brick and Dartmouth green shutters and doors has a history of building and burning. The building was constructed in 1784 – the date displayed around the clock under its short tower. This date makes the edifice the second oldest building on campus, trailing Webster Cottage by four years. Dartmouth Hall burned for the first time in 1904. It was rebuilt with sturdier materials around a cornerstone laid by the Sixth Earl of Dartmouth, a descendent of the namesake of the institution. Despite a second fire, the building still stood and housed the foreign language departments.

On some days, I would have left the Baker Library and headed to my right to go to the Sanborn House. The small, red brick building houses the English Department. Its small library is plush and wooden – a place for a person to sit and enjoy inspiration. I was such a person, and more than once, I sat in the library, writing and musing.

I enjoyed another activity a few times in the Sanborn House: afternoon tea. The house was endowed by an alumnus who asked that a tradition of a tea time be maintained in honor of Professor Edwin David Sanborn who made a practice of inviting undergraduate students to his home on Thursdays for tea.

My experience with the teas was outstanding. Faculty and students would gather semi-formally, or at least ritually, but with no defined agenda. They would talk about current events across the campus and around the world, and they would discuss their research. At one single tea, I learned what an asymptote was, I engaged in lively conversation about missions to Haiti, and I was inspired by a discussion to later read *The Old Man and the Sea* for the first time.

It was too early for tea, and I had another plan.

If you were to walk across the green towards Baker Library, you couldn't help but notice the formidable structure of Webster Hall. Massive but squat, with red brick and four pillars, Webster sits in the foreground and to the east of Baker. From the outside, it always struck me as imposing and secretive.

Webster Hall houses the Rauner Special Collections Library. The idea of a special collection at an Ivy League institution intrigued me. The college has massive libraries such as Baker and Berry, and various departments have specialized libraries, including the English library in the Sanborn House. With so many libraries, what qualifies as a special collection?

I walked in the front door of the library, marveling at how bright the inside appeared in contrast to its exterior. Only a few students or faculty members sat at the wooden tables poring over books. Whatever a special collection was, it did not seem to hold mass appeal at noon on a Tuesday.

I approached the information desk and explained who I was to an assistant, who retrieved a librarian for me. Once we got past the basic introduction to my project, he asked me, "So how can I help you?"

I suppose I could have answered any number of ways, but what I said was, "I'd like to see the coolest things you have in this library."

My librarian seemed like a diligent and intelligent guy. No matter what I would have requested, I think he would have provided a meaningful answer with a smile. My question, however, provided an opportunity for him to show off and to set the agenda according to his tastes.

Before we were done, several students and other librarians had joined us. We went on quite a journey. We looked at Daniel Webster's hat – alumnus, lawyer,

senator, Secretary of State, and apparent wearer of hats –
and other non-literary items of interest.

We turned to a glossed leaf bible from the 12ᵗʰ
century, just a couple of pages of handwritten text.

We looked at a collection of bookplates – decorative
labels placed inside a book to identify ownership – of
which the Rauner collection has tens of thousands,
including an especially rare plate carved by Paul Revere.

Next was a collection of incunabula. These works
were printed – not handwritten – prior to the 15ᵗʰ century.
The oldest was a Latin dictionary from 1470, and it was
the single oldest book in Dartmouth's library.

The Shakespeare collection, frankly, scared me. We
were looking at extremely rare, extremely old works. Some
of the volumes we examined were valuable beyond
accounting in financial terms, and I could see a special
reverie in the eyes of the librarians in the room as we
gazed on.

It is not an exaggeration to write that my favorite
pieces – the items that impacted me the most – related to
Dartmouth College itself. We looked at the charter for the
institution. Faint and stained, signed in 1769 by Sir John
Wentworth, governor of New Hampshire, the document
brought into being this place of such impact and import.

I have a small collection of yearbooks, and I was
glad to see a compilation of Sketches of the Alumni of
Dartmouth College. This document goes back to the first
class to graduate Dartmouth in 1771, and it provided
biographical detail for the alumni body. For example,
among the class of 1773 was John Smith, "the son of
Joseph and Elisabeth (Palmer) Smith, was born at Rowley,
Ms, Dec. 21, 1752, and died at Hanover, Apr. 30, 1809, ae
56. He studied divinity with the Rev. Pres. Eleazar
Wheelock, D.D. and was ordained to the ministry,
probably at Hanover; was tutor at Dart. Coll. from 1774 to
1778..." The printed text was annotated with handwritten
notes. In the case of John Smith, the first handwritten

note wondered whether his mother was born "Palmer," as printed, or "Sawyer."

The sketches are as varied and interesting as people are. Anyone who enjoys history and people – and certainly anyone who is interested in reading the obituaries of strangers – would find these works captivating.

Some of the most meaningful documents were those that referred to Dartmouth College as "Dartmouth University." A set of travel documents used to present the institution overseas to potential funders in the 1700s called the school a university. Both labels seemed to have been used at one point or another.

The reason I was interested in this is because I knew that Dartmouth is the only one of the eight Ivies that is designated a "college" as opposed to a "university," and I knew that this was a conscious choice. The term "university" implies more prestige – a higher level of research and learning. A university, for example, can have component colleges. In many places outside of the United States, the term "college" implies either technical training or a high school.

Dartmouth would certainly qualify as a university, so why does it cling to the college appellation?

The reason dates back to the early 19th century. The trustees of Dartmouth College fired its president, John Wheelock. Certain members of the government disagreed with the decision to dismiss Wheelock, so they staged a coup. They modified the charter of Dartmouth College, renaming it Dartmouth University, and changing its governance structure. They seized the charter and the buildings and began operating under a new legal entity.

The college continued with its mission in rented space off campus while it sued the "university treasure" for the return of the charter. The college, in this matter, was represented by Daniel Webster, and the matter was heard by the U.S. Supreme Court.

The college won the case in 1819, and the charter and buildings were returned to Dartmouth College.

Not that folks have first-hand memories of this, and acknowledging that it is hard to carry a burning grudge across generations, Dartmouth College chooses to be a college because its name was hard won. Despite the misperceptions that the term "college" may summon, Dartmouth will forever be proud to be Dartmouth College.

*

I started with Dartmouth on a pedestal. It thrived up there.

My project is about the people and places I experienced throughout my adventure. It is a subjective tale, and I recognize the butterfly effect that could have sent me down any number of divergent paths.

I am thankful and surprised at how well the stars aligned to bring me the experience I had at Dartmouth. The people were as quirky as they were anywhere, but I enjoyed a tremendous amount of luck. As glad as I was to leave the Experiment alive, I was sad to be leaving this community.

Had I not been so fortunate to be born with my last name, I would have considered changing it to Green. My experience at Dartmouth was that inspiring.

I left Hanover knowing that I had reached an apex of my experience. I did not know what awaited me at Yale, but my expectations were managed. I did not expect or even dream that I would have another experience like Dartmouth again.

YALE UNIVERSITY

Q: How many Yale students does it take to screw in a light bulb?

A: None – New Haven looks better in the dark.

Yale would be a crowning jewel in any community, but New Haven is a city that could use a jewel. It has a reputation for being dangerous and dirty. It has great pizza on Wooster Street, but I wouldn't want to walk the mile to get there at the wrong time of day.

But Yale is not New Haven. Yale is an urban campus – and like all urban, suburban, and rural campuses in America – there is always at least a threat of crime. Life at Yale, however, can be safe and sheltered. One can pursue an education and experience life with minimal exposure to danger if one chooses.

Prior to this exploration, my history with Yale was brief.

A few years earlier, I was deciding to which law schools I should apply. School snob that I am, I was aiming for the best schools, which to me, meant the Ivy League. Yale Law School offered many features that appealed to me – such as a small student body – but I was most intrigued because it was the highest-ranked law school in the country.

It should not be a surprise that I applied.

It also was not a huge surprise when I was rejected. I had a healthy record of academic and professional accomplishments, but Yale Law turns away similarly accomplished applicants regularly.

What was a surprise was the speed of the rejection. I mailed my application on a Monday, and it seemed like by Wednesday I was reading the rejection letter. It was almost as if they were sending a pre-emptive strike:

93

Dear Mr. Green:
We at Yale Law School understand that you are thinking of applying for admission to our next class. We urge you to reconsider. Harvard has a lovely program, and we are sure that you would be much happier there.

Yours (but not literally),
Guy Nameless

Perhaps it is a corollary of the Groucho Marx statement, "I don't want to belong to any club that will accept people like me as a member," but I arrived at Yale as a fan.

*

My project, for the most part, is a story about the people that I met in my travels. It is a rare and accomplished young person who finds herself studying at an Ivy League school.

As such, I would love to tell you about Linda – a Yale upperclassman who was invaluable to my project. Of course, I would change her name to protect her privacy, but we face another challenge in my effort to tell you about her:

I don't know much about her.

I encountered many students – helpful and horrible, wonderful and worrisome – but Linda was different. She adopted me and my cause. She facilitated various events and introduced me to dozens of her peers. On a day when things seemed to be slow, she would materialize with an invitation or suggestion. Most of what I know about Yale I learned through her and her network.

For all of her helpfulness, she was mysterious. When I would ask a question, she would find a classmate to answer it, but *she* would not typically answer it. I never

94

attended a class with her or saw her at a party. I did not know what her major was and I never saw her room.

Through talking to her and those to whom she referred me, I discovered that she was highly accomplished, incredibly modest, and prone to extreme secrecy. I can share two pieces of speculation about Linda.

The first is that her post-Yale plan was to work for the clandestine services of the United States. She had completed an internship with an agency in or near Washington, DC the preceding summer, and she was in the process of earning her security clearances to join the agency upon graduation. Whether she was practicing for her new career or whether her chosen profession was just especially well-suited for her, no one could say.

The second piece of speculation was that Linda was a member of one of the secret societies at Yale.

Secret societies are not unique to Yale. At Dartmouth, I walked by the Sphinx building often on my way to visit fraternities or to spend time with the athletes in the gym. During my time at Dartmouth, however, not one student referenced the Sphinx – the oldest secret society on campus – when talking to me. On the other hand, the very first student I met at Yale and many of those I met afterwards mentioned the secret societies.

Yale is home to many secret groups, but there are four that overshadow the others: Skull and Bones, Scroll and Key, Book and Snake, and Wolf's Head.

Even if students were not talking about the secret societies, it would be hard for me to ignore them. One look at the Skull and Bones tomb on High Street would pique the interest of any passerby. Considering that the two major contenders in the presidential election at the time of my visit were not just Yalies but members of the same secret society at Yale, I was quite curious about these organizations.

I could write an entire book about a secret society – but author Alexandra Robbins beat me to it with *Secrets of the Tomb,* and she did a better and more thorough job of it than I possibly could – so I will give just a few pertinent details here.

The first thing to know about the secret societies is that they are social groups. Just as a fraternity or club might bring people together, so do the secret societies. The secrecy gives rise to speculation and rumor about what the groups could be up to – that is part of the point of them – but at the heart of it, the answer seems to be that they are up to socially bonding with other students. They may do it over a taxidermied wolf's face for all we know, but the point is socialization.

Another point to be made is that the alumni of these societies are no joke. One of the advantages of any university is its alumni network. It gives job seekers and professional gold diggers a group of people with whom they share a point of similarity – an "in" to be leveraged professionally. The more connected and influential the alumni, the more valuable this asset. The Ivies boast an incredible alumni body in terms of power. Some Ivies outmatch others, with alumni at the highest levels of government and industry, and Yale is one of the institutions at the top of this pecking order. The alumni of the secret societies at Yale, however, are at the pinnacle of this power. Therefore, some of the most powerful alumni in all of the Ivy League are those who have spent time in these societies at Yale. And these alumni develop deep affinity for the members of their groups – deeper and more powerful than the bonds that develop between alumni in general. Thus, membership in a secret society leads to access to alumni who not only can provide professional assistance, but who are likely to want to help their younger brothers and sisters.

Despite the tangible advantages of participating in a secret society, not every student aspires to being nominated to one. I met many students who spoke negatively about the societies, stating that they would never want to be a part of one. Talking to a small group of undergraduates after a class, they more or less agreed that they would participate if they were tapped – the process through which juniors are picked for the societies in April of each year – but that they didn't feel strongly about being in one. Allowing for the distinct possibility that some students were psychologically preparing themselves to not be tapped, service in a secret society was not necessarily the ambition of every Yalie.

A final point: You may wonder how secret the societies are if I'm writing about them and everyone was talking about them. The answer is that they are not super-secret in some respects.

Tap week is a publically known and defined time period, when students are selected for secret societies. Watchful undergrads can detect signs that their peers either have been tapped or are out a-tapping others. Moreover, Thursday evening is the major activity night for secret societies – a time when they gather for dinner or incantations or animal sacrifices or quilting or whatever they do. If Steve has always been a member of your social set, eating dinner with you for three years, and suddenly he consistently skips dinner on Thursdays in his senior year, you may develop a suspicion that he is a part of a surreptitious group.

Or he wants you to think that he is, so he travels to nearby West Haven to have dinner and study alone every Thursday evening.

But not Linda. She was well connected with her peers and highly respected – everything that a secret society would want in a member. I cannot confirm that she was a member, of course, but she certainly should have been.

*

One area where Linda and her classmates provided invaluable help was in my exploration of the residential system at Yale.

I suppose if I had to identify the biggest difference between my college experience and the "typical" college experience, it comes down to where I lived. Academically, I was as involved as a person could be. In addition, I attended events, participated in extracurricular activities, and made friends and dated. But I never lived on campus or with other students.

The strength of the social bonds within a group – I believe – can be determined and described through a quasi-scientific formula that accounts for the proximity of the members, the duration of the shared experience, and the amount of adversity faced. A college student living in a suite with five classmates over multiple years, while studying and managing the social dramas of the late teens/early twenties, can expect to forge friendships and connections that last a lifetime.

An additional variable in the equation is the quality of the tools and space that they share. Three people living in a VW bus might have a different life than three people sharing a mansion with a swimming pool and grand piano. Differences between living spaces – holding all other variables as constant – can produce very different experiences.

A pivotal factor in the life of students at Yale College – the undergraduate academic unit of Yale University – is the residential colleges to which they are assigned. Every school that I had visited had dorms of various types, but I had never seen anything like the living situation at Yale.

There is no off-campus living of which to speak. Every freshman is assigned to one of 12 residential colleges. The assignments are random with the narrow exception that legacies – students who follow in the footsteps of their parents in attending Yale – can follow their footsteps into the same residential college. Once a student is affiliated with a house, it is theirs for the duration of their stay and a part of their brand for life.

If upon reading this, you start to conjure up images of the world of J.K. Rowling's Harry Potter – go ahead. I can tell you that the experience left me thinking of Hogwarts on a regular basis. Both Hogwarts and Yale are modeled after the system at Cambridge and Oxford in England, where the residential colleges nestle within the university.

Although freshmen are assigned to a college, they do not all move into them upon arrival. Members of 10 of the 12 colleges live on Old Campus as freshmen. This is – as the name implies – the oldest part of Yale's campus. The single oldest building on campus is Connecticut Hall, the last building standing of Old Brick Row – a series of similarly-designed Georgian buildings. In 1925, the university built an architectural twin for Connecticut Hall. The twin, McClellan Hall, was met with resistance by students and community members who felt that the second building marred the campus. They mocked the construction with the slogan, "For God, for Country, and for Symmetry." Today, Connecticut Hall is a meeting space and McClellan is one of several dorms in the immediate area housing Yale freshmen.

It would be neglectful if I did not address another dorm on Old Campus: Vanderbilt Hall. A son of Cornelius Vanderbilt, of railroad wealth and fame, attended Yale University in the 1890s. The son died as a junior, and Cornelius donated the money to build Vanderbilt Hall.

Two persistent rumors surround the dormitory.

The first is that the building is backwards. The intention, according to the story, is that the construction was supposed to face inwards towards the rest of Old Campus. The fact that the building faces outwards towards Chapel Street is attributed to builders who read the plans upside down. An apocryphal tale, but one a visitor might encounter when talking to students.

The second tale involves an opulent suite sitting over the archway of the building and overlooking Old Campus. The common room in the suite – with its rich wood floor and walls, grand (but not functional) fireplace, ornate chandelier, and bay window – and the similarly appointed bedrooms were designed as a living space for any Vanderbilt descendent who enrolled at Yale. The only problem is that decades passed with no Vanderbilt attending Yale. The year that Yale College began to admit female undergraduates, Vanderbilt Hall was designated a living space for females; but that same year, a male Vanderbilt enrolled at Yale. He sued for his right to live in the luxurious Vanderbilt Suite, and the university acquiesced. This self-proclaimed "luckiest man on campus" eventually met his bride at Yale – one of his neighbors in Vanderbilt Hall. So the story goes, at least.

Is this one poppycock? Or did I just win a $10 bet with a friend by appropriately working the word "poppycock" into this book?

Some parts of the story seem to be false. There was no male Vanderbilt heir who moved into the suite among the female students. There was no marriage that was born of this tale.

But here is the part that is true: There is a Vanderbilt Suite that is more lavish and magnificent than I can describe. I saw many amazing living spaces in my journey – and probably at least half of them were at Yale – but I never saw anything like this. Breathtaking, not only in its handsomeness, but in the fact that they let actual 21-year olds live there with their futons and second-hand chairs and mini-refrigerators. Any scholar who is assigned that space is a contender for the title of luckiest person on campus.

Old Campus is home to various activities for students ranging from the Freshmen Olympics to Commencement. I was not present at Yale for any major Old Campus events, but I spent time with the freshman class exploring the buildings and culture in this area. The newbie students slept at Old Campus, and they certainly developed friendships beyond their residential houses, but I had the distinct impression that they were passing the time before moving into their "real" houses the next year. They had access to their residential colleges, and I often encountered the freshmen there, studying in nooks, partaking in activities, or dining with their upperclassmen colleagues.

If students from 10 of the 12 colleges live on Old Campus as freshmen, I couldn't help but wonder what life was like for their classmates in the other two colleges.

I spent a weekend with members of Timothy Dwight College – or TD – who were extremely passionate about their house. The college has an official motto that resonates with me: Someday, perhaps, it will be pleasant to remember these things. It is the unofficial motto, however, that was most often quoted to me: Àshe, which translates from the West African language of Yoruba to English as "We make it happen." I was never clear what exactly they were making happen, but I admired their passion.

Speaking of passion, the students of TD seemed to share another appetite: The abuse of the other college that housed its members for all four years, Silliman College.

The students of TD claimed to have tighter bonds and a better experience than many of the other residential colleges due to the fact that students moved in as freshmen. They allowed for the possibility that Silliman College members had similar bonds, to the extent that viruses or weasels were capable of bonding.

Undergraduates, not unexpectedly, had the most affinity for their own colleges, but I found that the majority of students not affiliated with either TD or Silliman viewed those two houses as outsiders or afterthoughts. The price of not living on Old Campus was perhaps an otherness that could not be outgrown.

Sometimes being out of mind was not the worst thing. The colleges of Morse and Stiles were not forgotten; they were simply deemed worst by many students. These two most recent additions built in the 1960s are located a short, but significant, walk away from the rest of the campus. Their style is decidedly modern. They lack the history of some of the other houses that contain fourth or fifth generation legacies. Thus, as several Yalies told me, these two colleges are viewed as housing for students without the family connections to be placed in a better house. It is not an aspersion cast at individuals, but rather a stigma associated with the residential colleges themselves.

I explored many of the colleges and talked with dozens and dozens of students, and I found my house, if you will, in Branford College.

Branford and Saybrook Colleges were created in 1933 when the Memorial Quadrangle was divided into the two houses. The light colored but variegated stone work, the several chimneys, and the artificially cracked and repaired windows – all surrounding an interior courtyard of grass, trees, and benches – looks like a prototypical college living environment.

And, of course, there is Harkness Tower.

Harkness Tower is my favorite architectural feature of Yale. I love it for the symbolism and thought that went into it. It was one of the tallest freestanding structures at the time it was built – 216 feet, one foot for every year of Yale's existence at the time of its construction. It has four clock faces on the exterior and a 54-bell carillon on the interior. The gothic tower features a variety of carvings and statues. The lowest level represents eight of the most notable Yalies, including Nathan Hale, Jonathan Edwards, Samuel Morse, and Eli Whitney. Four figures depicting four classical Greek learners – Aristotle, Euclid, Homer, and Phidias – sit above these. The next level includes the allegorical figures for Medicine, Business, Law, Justice, the Church, Freedom, etc. The top of the tower is adorned with gargoyles representing Yale students: Athletes, scholars, and socialites. Lots of stone representing lots of ideas.

It isn't for everyone. A well-worn myth sometimes attributed to Frank Lloyd Wright – or other famous architects – is that he was asked where he would choose to be if he could be anywhere in the United States. He answered, "Harkness Tower at Yale, so I would not have to look at it."

Okay, maybe Harkness Tower is a bit much. But Yale is a bit much.

One peculiarity of residential life at Yale is the system of adults who oversee the houses and help to guide the students. Each house has its own dean. The deans are Yale faculty members who serve as the chief academic officers of the residential colleges. They personally advise and mentor the undergraduates who live within the college. They handle some paperwork – such as helping their pupils add or drop classes – but they also serve as advocates for students in dealing with instructors across the campus.

The other pivotal figure in the lives of Yale undergrads is the master. The master of each college is also a faculty member, but the masters are the chief administrative – as opposed to academic – officers of the colleges. The master and his or her family lives in an apartment within their residential college. The college is their home, and the families regularly dine with students in the college eateries. The masters are responsible for the well-being of their students, and they help to shape the culture of the house through social and educational offerings.

An interesting activity in Branford and throughout the residential system is the Masters' Teas. These monthly-ish events often transpire in the apartment of the master. Speakers and honored guests are invited to speak

103

with students and entertain questions. The guests of honor are authors, political figures, recipients of major awards, activists, and humanitarians. The power of these speakers in such an intimate setting adds a valuable dimension to Yale life.

I attended teas in several colleges – including Pierson, Jonathan Edwards, and, of course, Branford. While at Yale, I sat in on perhaps seven courses, all of which were recommended to me. I learned about Yale and Yale students in those courses, and I learned a bit about the subject matter along the way. At the teas, however, I felt like I received an *education* on the topic, whatever the topic happened to be. For anyone who wants to learn from enthralling experts, I would recommend the Masters' Teas.

With Linda's introductions, I spent a great deal of time in Branford College. I hiked up the stairs of Harkness Tower and met with the team charged with playing the carillon. I explored the bedrooms with their bench seats in front of windows overlooking the courtyard or views of Sterling Memorial Library. I was fascinated by the fireplaces – an inspiring accent in a college room. I sat in the two-story library among thousands of books at the disposal of any Branford student. I ate many meals with students in the dining hall in the college – three-story ceilings, huge chandeliers, bright oversized windows, and some of the best food I ate on any campus. Under the dining hall was the common room. This massive room served as a movie room with a screen and projector, a music room with a piano, and a meeting room with community members hosting events.

If that were the end of residential life, I could walk away impressed; but I haven't even gotten to the good part yet:

The basement. That is where life happens.

Branford's basement has *two* courts that can be used for basketball or squash. Every time I saw the courts in use, however, someone was dancing on them. Either a class had been formed or a person or group was practicing. It was social, but the students I saw were always hard at work.

Similarly, the basement contains an art studio with everything an artist might want – except, perhaps, sunlight. I never met an art major in the basement studio, but I did see it in use. Students from an assortment of majors and backgrounds would work on projects in their spare time. I was told that the art majors had even better spaces in which to work on campus.

Next to the art studio is the pottery studio. It had gone through a period of atrophy and disuse, collecting trash and junk. The master wrote to the students and asked them what they wanted to do with the space. A junior, Sharon, responded and said that it should be left as a pottery room. The master assigned her to take charge of the project. He invested by buying new potter's wheels. Sharon did her part by inviting the men's rugby team to use the room. The men discovered that throwing pots could be fun, and the room had been in use ever since.

Sharon showed me the room as she was telling the story. A few women were in the process of using the equipment in the room. One was glazing what she described as "a big goofy plate." Another was crafting four female statues to use in a short film. One woman was learning to throw a pot as she took a break from writing her senior thesis. Another girl was coaching her at the wheel. It was not the scene from *Ghost* – it was more like the mashed potato scene in *Close Encounters of the Third Kind* – but it was inspiring to see these students engaged in such unusual artistry.

The Buttery – or "the Butt" – is a snack bar that is only open late at night. It is run by undergrads who serve up burgers, fries, chicken tenders, and milkshakes at midnight.

A game room, a laundry, computer lab, study spaces, gym – even a printing press – reside in the basement under Branford.

Now here's the kicker: Branford is one of 12 residential colleges. They all have these spaces. They have dining halls and bedrooms and common rooms and libraries. But they also have basements. Some have rock climbing walls; some have recording studios; some have video arcades; some have theaters; some have gourmet kitchens. Furthermore, the university offers resources beyond the residential colleges. Just as the art majors work in better studios, so are there better music spaces and athletic facilities and libraries.

Yale is simply an amazing place, and I am grateful to have had an opportunity to explore it.

*

"Oh, we're gay, all right," said the six foot ten basketball player.

We were sitting in Mory's, a private dining club in New Haven and an essential piece of Yale culture.

The statement seemed to be a non sequitur. "Oh," I responded casually, nodding towards his equally giant friend wedged into the table beside him. "Are you two a couple, then?"

He looked at me with confusion. "No! *We're* not gay." He cast a too-long arm around the room, "Yale is gay. Didn't you know that?"

I suppose I was expecting a punchline, but instead he said something that I would hear over and over again at Yale: "One in four Yale students are gay."

It wasn't that people said that a large proportion of Yale undergraduates were gay, or that 25% of Yale men were homosexual. The oft repeated slogan was "One in four Yale students are gay."

Digging deeper, I found that the common belief was that this statement only applied to the male population at Yale. Not that there wasn't a gay female population, but – whatever their numbers – it was outside of the one-in-four statistic.

Yale students would most often quote the statistic to me while explaining that Yale was the most liberal Ivy. This was a point of pride for many of the people that I met.

Liberal-ness is a tough attribute to measure. Perhaps it was a self-fulfilling prophesy, and I am sure that it had more to do with the people with whom I surrounded myself, but every school I had visited seemed very liberal. Honestly, I saw no signs that Yale was any more or less liberal than, say, Brown.

But the truth of the matter is not nearly as interesting to me as the fact that insiders in droves were making the statement. The same sentiment holds on the one-in-four rule. Was this measured at some point? Can we hang our collective hats on this fact? Did my observations even bear this out? No, on all counts. To be at Yale, however, was to be at a place that believed it was liberal.

Talking to students about this led me to think about diversity and the mythos of the Ivy League.

One area of misconception is that the Ivy League is a boys' club. Yale is not that.

It wasn't all that long ago, however, that it was. Until 1969, Yale College did not admit female undergraduates. This was not uncommon among top tier private schools, and several changed their policies around this time. In fact, many of the Ivies had "sister" schools for social events. Yale's Sister Ivy was Vassar College – a top-tier private institution that only admitted women until it, too, changed its policies in 1968 and began enrolling men.

One of the more spectacular art pieces at Yale is the *Women's Table*. Situated on the stone walk outside of the massive structure of Sterling Library, it was designed by a two-time alumna of Yale, Maya Lin. Lin may be best known for being the designer of the Vietnam Veterans Memorial in Washington, D.C. – a piece that she earned the honor of creating while she was a 21-year old undergraduate at Yale. The *Women's Table* is smooth granite cut into a round table. Carved into the stone is an outwardly spiraling series of numbers. The earliest number – representing the number of women at Yale in 1704 – is a zero. The second number for 1705 is also a zero. The zeros go on and on, until the space representing year 1873. This was thought to be the first year that the School of Fine Arts admitted women – although it was later discovered that the school admitted at least a couple of women in 1869. The numbers on the table increase significantly when the Yale School of Nursing opened in 1923, and again in 1969 when Yale College went co-ed. The numbers stop at 1993 when the monument was dedicated.

On a hot summer day, cool water flows over the surface of the table, attracting both the hot and the curious. In the winter of my visit, there was no water, but the structure served as a gathering point for community events such as Take Back the Night. It was a reminder that while Yale may be liberal, it had evolved into its current disposition.

Not only did many people believe that Yale was a boys' club, they also believed that Yale was a white boys' club.

Universities report statistics on the subject of the diversity of their applicants and enrolled students. One has only to look at these reports to know that Yale does have a student body that includes members of many marginalized groups. I can report that I met many students at Yale who self-identified as representing minority groups.

I was especially struck at Yale by the number of Asian and Asian American students.

I grew up in a suburban community that was a combination of Irish, Italian, Polish, and African American. Moreover, my time in the military exposed me to people of various backgrounds. But one group that I had perhaps been underexposed to was people of Asian descent.

At a house on Crown Street one evening, I attempted to explore this community by attending a meeting of the Asian Student Alliance, or ASA.

It is a good time to remind you that my project was not an undercover sting operation. I was not a professional field journalist attempting to blend into the background. I was an outsider by age and affiliation.

At the ASA meeting, I had another reason to stick out. I sat in a downstairs living room with several men and dozens of women representing a wide range of Asian ethnicities. Many of the attendees were members of Yale groups for specific Asian ethnicities. For example, the friend who invited me to the event was the president of the Filipino Club. Chinese, Thai, Indian, Korean, Taiwanese, Vietnamese, Japanese, Pakistani, Cambodian, Bangladeshi, and one Irish guy.

This was a good night to visit the ASA, I was told, because it was election night for the organization. Not only would there be a good turnout, but I would have an opportunity to hear the speeches and questions and answers.

The candidates made short speeches outlining their visions for Asian and Asian American students at Yale. Among the points made was the claim that one-in-eight Yale students self-identified as Asian or Asian American – Yalies love their one-in- statistics, apparently – but the College only offered two Asian-American Studies courses to undergraduates. The speeches were informative and occasionally inspirational.

My favorite speech, however, was from a freshman running for secretary. He, with great confidence, simply said, "I don't know much or have many ideas, but here I am!"

After each speech, the candidates were asked questions by the moderator – my Filipino friend – and by the audience. The questions were not ground balls. One of the recurring themes was to ask the candidates how they would get the attention of Yale administrators or the student community who, according to the crowd, appeared to be apathetic.

Ballots were distributed, votes cast in secret, collected, and tallied. Good news for the candidates: They all won. Fortunately for all of them, there was no opposition to any candidate or seat.

Sitting in on this event, I was again reminded of the complexity of my project. People are inherently complex, but Yale and other Ivy League students are more complicated due to their intelligence, ambition, and opportunities. At a glance, it might be tempting to label a student as "Asian" or "gay" or "female" or "athlete" or "chemistry major." But a single scholar can be all of these things and so much more.

*

Part of my project was meeting with as many students as possible. Students – like all people – come in various flavors. Some are kind and some are rude. Some had an agenda to pursue through me. Some actually had an air of danger or evil about them. Occasionally, I would meet with an undergrad and think to myself, "Wow – this is a horrible person!" or "So *that's* what a sociopath looks like!" It was rare, but it happened at least once at most schools.

At Yale, it happened when I met Stuart.

He reached out, offering to share his take on the school with me. We met at Au Bon Pain adjacent to the campus in New Haven because he wanted to ensure privacy. He had information to share, he said, but he wanted to do it away from prying eyes.

Stuart seemed to distrust the world around him while maintaining the utmost confidence in himself. His style of dress was bold with loud colors and clashing patterns. He was wrinkled and semi-untucked, but he carried himself in a way that led me to believe that his nerdy, disheveled demeanor was deliberate. Perhaps it was a disguise to further obstruct those who would attempt to listen in.

"You're Sean-Michael," he told me when he approached the table at which I was already sitting. I didn't disagree with him. "Switch me seats."

We circumnavigated the table so he could better watch the door.

"You want my take on Yale, so I'm going to give it to you," said Stuart. And so he did.

In summary, here is the problem with Yale: Too many gays, gentiles, and women.

The problem with New Haven: The blacks and Hispanics.

The problem with Au Bon Pain: The pain. *Pas bon du tout*, according to Stuart.

This young man was a racist, a misogynist, a homophobe, and hater of gluten. He was a freshman approaching his first set of finals in college, and he confessed to having (or needing) very few friends on campus. He had the world figured out. He was right and those who were different from him were wrong.

"Gee, well, okay," I said, standing to make my escape. "Thanks for taking the time."

"Wait!" he said. "We're not done."

"Err ... yes we are," I stated as I started to back away.

"Hey," he yelled, standing and puffing up to his full five feet, four inches, "I said we're not done." That which I suppose he intended as a threat resonated as a whine.

As I walked away, passing an employee of the restaurant on the phone, presumably with the police department, Stuart issued a loud rant directed at me. He predicted that my book was funded by the Pope, and I was on a mission to make African Americans and homosexuals look good.

"Put this in your book!" he shrieked as I reached the door. "Don't gloss over the problems with this place! Tell them what I told you!"

Well, Stuart, there you go. I hope that wisdom, self-awareness, and tolerance found you by your nineteenth birthday.

*

One of the biggest rivalries in the Ivy League is on exhibition at the Harvard v. Yale football game each fall. It is not just a football game; it is *the Game*.

The rivalry has been a tradition since 1875, when football was much more akin to rugby. Of course, the sport has changed – most significantly at the hands of a Yalie, Walter Camp, who proposed that each play begin at a "line of scrimmage" behind which the team had uncontested possession of the ball.

Each year, Harvard and Yale face each other in an event that draws massive crowds of students and alumni. The tailgate starts the Friday preceding the Game, and it ends sometime after the Game does.

I left New Haven bound for Cambridge on the afternoon of a Friday in mid-November, eager to see the festivities. I arrived at Harvard later than I intended, hopelessly lost on the streets of Boston, and I rushed into the event that I came to see: An a cappella showdown between Harvard and Yale.

I like football just fine, but collegiate singing . . . well, *there's* something to get excited about!

I stood in a Victorian great room with three elaborate chandeliers and carved woodwork throughout the space. The audience seemed to include few students. In fact, most of the students seemed to be members of the Duke's Men of Yale University. They were dressed in button down shirts with the cuffs turned up and brightly colored ties. One of the Duke's Men, Samuel, caught my eye and nodded to me from across the room. He was the undergrad who invited me to this pre-game event. I felt horrible that I had missed their part of the show.

Harvard's Din and Tonics were in the limelight and singing their guts out. They wore black tuxedos, complete with tails, with white shirts, ties, and vests. They were great showmen, responding enthusiastically when the audience called for an encore. They retook the stage and did a rendition of *Putting on the Ritz* that seemed appropriate in context.

I caught up with Samuel as he and his compatriots sold CDs in the back of the room, sharing space with the Dins. After profusely apologizing, I asked him if he knew the other folks in the room.

"Well, lots of the audience is our parents." With that, he signaled to an older gentleman who made his way towards us. "This is my dad, Bob."

"So what did you think of the concert?" I asked Bob.

"The singing was great," he began. Then he lowered his tone and whispered, "But the vibe in here is odd."

When he said that, I realized that something had been gnawing at me, but I didn't know what it was. "How so?" I asked.

He cast about with his eyes, making subtle head gestures. "Look at Them and look at Us."

And that's when I realized that there was a definite Them and Us.

Them was dressed formally – not just the singers, but the parents as well. The women among Them wore large pieces of jewelry over ball gowns. The members of

113

Them clung to each other as old friends who were perhaps once close, but who have been away from each other too long. They embraced, talked loudly, and clustered in the room.

Us was dressed in sweaters or tie-less dress shirts – including Bob in his blue fuzzy sweater – and the women were comfortably and confidently attractive. While Us talked to others of our kind, we were also comfortable ambling off to the bar ourselves.

As a person exploring the differences between the Ivies, I was interested to see the room divided fairly neatly into two groups. It could be that the members of the two parties had other engagements around the edges of the a cappella concert, thus accounting for the differences in dress, but it was a definite divide.

The next day, I joined Samuel, Bob, and hundreds of other Yale families and alumni for the tailgate party outside of Harvard Stadium – a 30,000-seat u-shaped structure across the Charles River from Cambridge. There were grills and drinks and laughing and celebration – everything you would expect from a tailgate – but it had a measure of civility and sophistication that I do not often think of when I imagine tailgates. Less camouflage dress and more luxury vehicles.

I was captivated by some of the shirts and slogans I saw that day.

One of the most popular shirts simply said across the chest, "Harvard sucks." The back read, "Princeton doesn't matter."

Two women – I guessed they were mother and daughter – wore T-shirts that bragged, "Yale ladies: rejecting Harvard boys since 1969."

I saw one father wearing a shirt that confused me at first. He was in the Yale section of the tailgate, but at a glance his shirt looked like a Harvard slogan. And then I read closer: "Harvard Utility Company: Producing tools since 1636."

I saw a few Yale students, some of whom I knew, toting crimson Harvard T-shirts. I barely registered the oddity, and I didn't ask anyone about it.

In another case of Us and Them, I did not see similar slogans among the Harvard families. Lots of institutional pride – they were a sea of crimson – but the wittiest slogan I saw demanded, "Beat Yale."

The tailgate may have been a blast, but the Game was a blowout. Harvard crushed Yale 35-3. It was not close; it was not pretty. What their T-shirts lacked in wit they made up for with effectiveness. I drove back to New Haven feeling the loss.

Monday rolled around and I stopped in the Sterling Memorial Library at Yale to check my e-mail. I had one – a cryptic one, of course – from Linda. All it said was: "You need to find Michael Kai and David Aulicino to talk about what happened on Saturday."

As a long-term visitor, my nerves were always a bit frayed. I was not trained as a journalist, and I had little experience chasing a story. More importantly, I lacked the thick skin and callous demeanor of a true member of the media. The nightmare that plagued me most often was that I would cause damage or step on toes during the course of my investigation.

I racked my memory trying to figure out what I could have done wrong at the Game.

I suppose going into this project and throughout it, I was seeking a quality spawned by naïveté. I was never an undergraduate at a school such as Yale – or a traditional aged or situated undergraduate anywhere – and I was seeking an ideal of the Ivy League. On some level, I was expecting students with surnames such as Kennedy or DuPont who were sipping martinis while studying furiously. I was looking for the prototypical Ivy League rites.

One such rite was that of the prank. Something clever and complicated. A prank where no one gets hurt, but everyone stops and marvels at the planning and scale of the caper. The pumpkin atop the McGraw Tower at Cornell – that's what I was looking for. Or maybe something from the classic movie, *Real Genius*.

Only when I connected with Mike and Dave did I discover that I was in the presence of such a prank and never knew it. The three of us sat down in the Pierson Dining Hall, named after the first rector of the University who was instrumental in the founding of Yale in 1701. We occupied a corner of a long table, the two pranksters sitting in a church pew facing me.

During the game, Mike and Dave executed their plan with the help of 20 of their Yale classmates. They all donned Harvard T-shirts and went to the Harvard alumni section of the spectating crowd, presenting themselves as the "Harvard Pep Squad." They eagerly passed out placards – some white, some red – down the rows of seats, telling the crowd that when the placards were held up all at once, it would spell, "Go Harvard."

Several times, this pep squad inspired the crowd to lift the signs, proudly displaying the message, "We suck."

These two geniuses were typical Yale seniors, casually dressed, thinking in the short-term about fall finals and in the long-term about graduate school. They have the distinction of being two of only three students in this book mentioned under their actual names. Not only are their names public record – which you will see when you look up the pictures of the prank, and I strongly recommend that you do – but their accomplishment is so great that they deserve the credit.

Well done!

*

My last days at Yale were spent in the basement of Branford and in the study rooms of Sterling Memorial Library. I tried to stay quiet and inconspicuous as my new friends studied, wrote, composed, and built. As students finished their last finals, with just a handful of hugs and goodbyes to their friends, they slipped away for home, leaving their colleagues to fend for themselves. Somewhere in the middle of this time, I took my leave, too.

One of the angina-inducing aspects of my project was the uncertainty of what to expect on each campus. I began with preconceptions or prior experiences. I arrived at schools with an outline of a plan, a sketch of areas to explore or resources to draw upon. Reality, however, rarely respects an outline, and preconceptions do not always hold up. I did not know, hour by hour, what would come next or how I would fare through it all.

I was a bit nervous about Yale. As I talked to friends at other schools, I sometimes mentioned my apprehension about Yale. They seemed confused by my hesitation, and they often reassured me that Yale students were great.

As I write this, I can still appreciate my initial concern better than I can articulate it. It was a concern about me, not Yale. Maybe it was the law school rejection or maybe it was the strong brand of Yale, but I felt inferior for the first time in this project. I was concerned that I would be more out of place at Yale than I would be at other schools. I felt that I might not be good enough.

I discovered an amazing and welcoming place. Yale dazzled me with the investment it makes in its buildings, opportunities, and people. The students were funny and smart and motivated. They brought me in and showed me what makes the institution so great. It is their graciousness that I will always remember.

Halfway done, and the safety and comfort of the University of Pennsylvania right around the corner.

The Things I Learned in College

THE UNIVERSITY OF PENNSYLVANIA

Q: How many Penn students does it take to change a light bulb?

A: One – but he gets six credits for it.

The University of Pennsylvania, or Penn, is the second largest and fourth oldest Ivy League school – and the only one to be founded by an American hero as noteworthy as Benjamin Franklin. Nestled into a neighborhood on the west side of Philadelphia, it is a campus of incredible beauty. The campus feels like an oasis within the neighborhood.

Penn operates on a system of course units rather than credits. The common perception is that the system benefits students who may be able to accumulate points towards graduation faster at Penn than they could at another institution.

I quite deliberately scheduled the University of Pennsylvania visit to follow the holiday break. I had started enough spring terms in my life to know the malaise of returning to school. After a holiday, it can be tough to get back in the swing of academic life. I wanted to pick an institution that would offer me a soft landing.

With the exception of Cornell, there could be no softer landing for me than Penn. I am from Pennsylvania, albeit the other side of the state. Anywhere in Pennsylvania feels like home to me, and I would only have to drive across the commonwealth following the break at the holiday. In addition, one of my best friends from childhood had attended Penn for two graduate degrees, and I spent a great deal of time with him on and near the campus.

More to the point: I earned a master's degree at Penn. Nerd that I am, I went to Penn for the sheer challenge of it immediately after I earned my undergraduate degree. I enrolled in a master's program that required me to take graduate-level courses in multiple departments and complete a capstone thesis that tied my research together. I tested myself further by trying to explore subjects that I had never tackled before.

For example, I would walk in on the first day of a graduate seminar in anthropology and sit among eight graduate students who had majored in anthropology as undergrads. They were pursuing doctorates in the subject. I, having never taken an anthro course previously, had to catch up to my classmates and then compete throughout the rest of the course. My idea of a good time.

During my time as a Penn student, I made plenty of friends, spent hours walking around campus, and was in and out of many buildings. It was comfortable and familiar for me.

When I arrived on campus in January, I had only been away for five years. I was practically guaranteed a happy experience.

*

One of my strategies on each campus was to contact the student-run newspaper and inform them about my project. At Cornell, this strategy earned me access to Greek life; at Dartmouth, it provided a place to live; and at Yale, it gave me contact with student groups. I received dozens of e-mails upon the publication of an article. Students would write and invite me to activities, professors would write to invite me to classes, and parents would write asking me to have their sons call home if I bumped into them.

The Penn article earned me all of that and more when it was published – a month after I left campus.

We'll return to this later.

*

Another tried and true strategy was the campus tour. At each school, I went on multiple tours of the campus. It was a great way to learn about the university and to avoid getting lost. Most importantly, it exposed me to some of the most outgoing and enthusiastic students. Tour guides – for the most part – are carefully chosen based on their personalities. Schools seek natural cheerleaders – people who cannot help but to exude love for their institutions. Some of the best people I met in the Ivy League were the tour guides who informed me and aided me along the way.

This tactic proved to be fairly successful at Penn. I met talented undergrads who were kind, sharp, and knowledgeable.

On the other hand, this tactic also led me to meet Barry.

My best friend, Shawn Hogan, drove out to Philadelphia to visit me for a few days on this leg of my journey. Shawn grew up six houses away from me, and we have been friends since I was two years old. We have had many adventures together, but our lives are very different – and the most significant difference between us is that he never chose to attend college. He is a successful business owner and a snappy dresser, but he has never shown any interest in earning a degree.

Even Shawn, however, had heard the myths about Penn and the other Ivies – perhaps from me. As I spoke with him about my project over the holiday, I could hear that under his questions were visions of unrivaled wealth and unsurpassed intelligence in the hands of beautiful, young people.

I wanted to dazzle Shawn, but I also wanted to give him a taste of the work in which I was engaged. I figured the first logical step would be the official campus tour.

The tours at Penn start at the Admissions Office in College Hall. The building is not only the oldest structure on the campus, but it is also quasi-famous. Shawn took one look at the stone front of the building, and, without prompting and despite the sunny day, he said, "I've seen this building on TV before, right?"

It is true that the stone front of the building with its entryway porch and faux towers looks very much like the house from *The Addams Family* show. It is also true that the creator of *The Addams Family* – Charles Addams – attended Penn, although he allegedly denied using the campus building as an inspiration.

Shawn seemed appropriately awestruck by the history.

We walked to the stone courtyard behind College Hall. We waited with approximately a dozen prospective Penn students and their collective families outside the Admissions Office.

Barry, our tour guide, emerged from the building. He wore sandals and a short-sleeved pastel polo shirt despite the freezing February temperature. He collected us, and began leading us across the courtyard. Before we left the shadow of College Hall, he stopped, reoriented himself, and set out in a new direction. Less than a minute later, he slowed while arguing with himself. He spun, surveying the landscape and with a loud, "Fuck it!" he reversed course again.

One of the most unusual aspects of the tour was the fact that Barry never made an attempt to learn about his audience. He asked no questions of us. The tour and the commentary were going to happen no matter whom – or if anyone – heard it.

He led us towards the Graduate School of Fine Arts, walking backwards and acknowledging the sights. I was admittedly only half paying attention when I heard him say, "This is where you can find the sluttiest girls." I saw some of the parents pull their sons and daughters a bit closer, and I saw Shawn note the location. Barry did not seem to notice any reaction.

When we came to the Engineering quad, Barry stated that he had intended to study engineering but that he could not handle the math. He stopped and said, "Come on, I'll show you where the dumb kids go." Then he led us back the way we had come.

I tried to engage him with a few questions. I inquired, "What percentage of the student body participates in Greek life?"

His non-statistical response: "I'm in the only decent frat on campus. The rest of those kids are all losers."

He went on to tell me, Shawn, and all of the parents and prospective students on the tour that his fraternity was having a party that evening for "all the rich kids" at Penn.

We never made it far enough up Locust Walk to get to one of the most significant academic units at Penn: The Wharton School. Instead, with the brand new Huntsman Hall looming in front of us in the distance, Barry changed course again and took us back to College Hall where we disbanded in a bit of confusion. I overheard a father and mother debating whether or not to go into Admissions to complain.

Shawn turned to me and asked, "Is that *really* the tour that they use to convince people to come here?"

"Yeah, what did you think?"

He considered the question. "I suppose it would be good for anyone who identifies with being rich, dumb, and slutty. But it really would have to be all three."

"Why?"

"Well, I fall under two of those categories," he responded, "and I'm not impressed."

*

A few days before that tour, I sat in on a sociology class. It was a large class, taught by a full professor. It also had recitation sections staffed by a fleet of teaching

123

assistants – graduate students who were paid to help a professor by leading additional discussions about the material. Sociology as a subject to explore at Penn came recommended, but I chose this particular course more or less at random.

The size of the room made the lecture feel a bit impersonal, and I found myself struggling to stay connected to the professor's words. From my vantage point, I could see a few classmates around the room engaged in the same struggle.

I sat in the proximity of two students who were whispering about a party scheduled later in the week. I ended up drawn into the conversation, and we talked a bit about my project. They invited me to the party, which they referred to as a fraternity party. As one of the students, C.J., wrote down the address, I asked, "Are you sure this is okay? You don't need to check with the fraternity first?"

C.J. looked up from his scrawling and said with a smile, "It's fine. I'm the president of the fraternity."

I looked at him and realized that I had unfairly stereotyped him. His skateboard occupied the seat between us, and his purple hair was stuffed under a watch cap with a skull logo on it. He had several visible piercings, including a large spike through his lip that caused him to punctuate every fourth word or so with a sucking sound. To my eye, he did not look like a fraternity leader, nor did he look like a Penn student. But he was both, and I imagined that a party with C.J. at the helm was likely to be a different experience than the parties I had encountered in my journey thus far.

Shawn and I arrived at 11 p.m. at the address that C.J. provided. I was concerned at first because the fraternity house was not where I expected to find one. Many Greek societies line Locust Walk. These quaint houses are burrowed into the heart of the campus. On a nice day, fraternity brothers and sorority sisters can be seen from the Walk having cook-outs or playing volleyball, or they may set up stands beside the Walk to distribute literature for campus events or to conduct fundraising activities for charitable causes. Not all of Greek life was this centrally located, but the houses were grand and well-marked with Greek lettering. There was a *feel* to the houses.

On this night, however, we pulled up in front of a house on Pine Street. The house was nondescript and quiet, surrounded by similarly sleepy neighbors. The lights were on, though, and there was a cardboard sign on the porch with Greek characters hastily painted on, so we took a chance and pushed through the door.

As we went in, I saw C.J. preparing to leave. He needed to run a quick errand, he stated. He seemed uncomfortable being caught by us in the offing. He slipped by us, telling us to mingle and enjoy the party.

Shawn and I stood in a bit of confusion. I didn't know where to start. I wasn't sure that I would know anyone else, but no one else was even in sight. The house was narrow and we could see from the front door to the kitchen; but it was tall, so we began to ascend into uncertain terrain.

We encountered more young people upstairs clustered in various rooms. They seemed understandably suspicious of us. Our age, dress, and lack of facial piercings identified us as outsiders. They, on the other hand, made C.J. look like a Wall Street broker.

I had a conversation with a couple of the brothers about the fraternity. They admitted women into their society, although it was against the rules, so they hid this fact from both the university and their national headquarters. They said that their membership was fifty-percent female, but I saw only one woman in the house that night.

The house, it turned out, was not their regular house. Their fraternity was suffering some setbacks. They told us they were trying to earn their way back onto

125

campus after being kicked off for an incident involving illegal drugs.

Whatever written notice they received saying they were kicked off campus, I can only assume that they smoked it.

On some subjects I am hopelessly naïve. When I lived in the Experiment at Dartmouth, my housemates had to educate me on the pungent smell that clung to every piece of fabric in the house. I don't know much about drugs, but I know more after attending this party. Marijuana was the tamest thing we saw being ingested that night, but we saw it being ingested through various devices, ranging from old fashioned joints to bongs to hookahs to model airplanes. One student apologized profusely to me for the lack of cocaine. Shawn was offered a plastic bag filled with paint thinner to breathe out of, and I literally checked the pulses on two unconscious – perhaps sleeping – people.

After being in the house for just seven minutes or so, I grew too nervous to stay. Research or no research, I was concerned about how I would explain our presence during a DEA raid. Therefore, I closed up my notebook, grabbed my friend, and ran from the house.

That was the only party I attended in my first 30 days at Penn.

*

While visiting Cornell University, I was not often reminded that there was another Cornell – Cornell College, located in Mount Vernon, Iowa. A fine school, I am sure, but not an Ivy League school by location, academic reputation, or football conference.

My point is that one could attend four years of school in Ithaca and never know that there is another school a thousand or so miles away with a strikingly similar name.

126

The University of Pennsylvania has a different issue. It is confused so often with the Pennsylvania State University that it has spawned an assortment of clarifying T-shirts, often with the university seal and the legend, "Not Penn State."

Part of the value in choosing an Ivy League school is for the brand recognition. When a person hears that you attended Harvard, they may make assumptions about your intelligence, work ethic, or financial wherewithal. The assumptions may not be true, but they are often welcome. Just as those who drive Bentleys are often happy to be recognized as those who drive Bentleys, and may be quietly or vocally disappointed when their car is confused with a Chrysler.

Hence the angst of Penn students and families when acquaintances remark, "Oh, my cousin went to Penn State!" Or the torment when a friend says, "I considered going into the agriculture program at Penn." Or the frustration when a stranger at a rest area, upon observing the Penn window sticker on your car, remarks, "Your team is looking great this year. Go Nittany Lions!"

Part of the confusion – for better or worse – is that Penn State is a great school, too. It is a research institution located a few hours west of Philadelphia. It has great academics, sports, and people. We should all be so lucky as to be mistaken for Penn State students, right?

For the relative few of us who earned an opportunity and made a choice to study at an Ivy League school, however, we wish that people could tell us apart.

*

Sometimes on my trip, things went well. In the case of the University of Pennsylvania, I was indebted to the mysterious Linda at Yale once again.

Linda gave me another gift as I left Yale before the break. She said she would put me in touch with her friend, Gretchen, at Penn. Sure enough, a couple of weeks in, Gretchen reached out to me and we agreed to meet in Houston Hall over crepes.

I parked with some trepidation on 42nd Street, well to the west of the campus. Parking can be tough in any urban area. Finding a spot on the street can be hard, and off-street parking gets expensive fast.

In this case, I found a spot on the street in front of a broken meter. I don't mean to imply that meter was defective as much as it was more or less missing. A short, metal post wore a piece of a parking meter like a hat. There was no place to insert a quarter or a gauge to show the time remaining.

Parking enforcement is no joke in West Philly, but a broken meter seemed like a blessing. A legal space with no way to pay for it – I'll take it!

For good measure, I placed a large, handwritten note in my windshield that read, "Broken meter – please do not ticket!"

It was not the best defense, but it was what I had.

I set off on foot. I walked down Locust Street, passing houses that held students and locals alike. When I crossed 40th Street and Locust Street became Locust Walk, I instantly relaxed a notch. It was as if I traversed an invisible line of demarcation. I was no longer in West Philadelphia; I was at the University of Pennsylvania.

I walked through an area of residential housing. The huge high rises of Rodin, Harrison, and Harnwell College Houses loomed over the Walk and some smaller housing options in this section of campus. The gigantic skyscrapers house hundreds of students in apartments – many of which include kitchens, and many of which offer coveted views of Philadelphia. These buildings offer more than just housing. These are spaces for *living*. They have work out rooms, music rooms, computer labs, cafés, study spaces, and lounges. They are spaces with many young people crammed inside, for better or worse, but they offer options beyond television or sleep.

My last trip inside one of these buildings had been several years earlier in the company of a friend who was an undergraduate living in Harrison College House while I lived off campus. He proudly referred to himself as a HRP pronounced "herp" – a high-rise person. My clearest memory of Harrison was the distinct smell of Ramen Noodles smacking me in the face every time I stepped off of the elevator onto his floor.

At this point on my trip, I had not been back inside to see if it had changed.

The residential hall that I was most eager to explore, however, was the Quadrangle, commonly called the Quad. This was campus living more in tune with my vision of the Ivy League.

For one thing, it is a charming building to behold. Construction started in 1895, and it was complete in 1928, more or less. I discovered in my travels – particularly at Yale – that I am a fan of gothic architecture, and the Quad is as gothic as it gets with its red brick and elaborate details. My favorite of those details on the outside are the 163 individually designed gargoyles perched upon the roofs of the structure. They are not just fun to look at, but they are also functional, helping to route rainwater from the roof.

Beyond the look of the place, I admire it for its size. The walls stretch from 36th Street to 38th Street. A large archway sits under Memorial Tower, built to memorialize the Penn alumni who served in the Spanish-American War. Upon passing through the archway, one can begin to appreciate the scale of the Quad. An expansive green space is surrounded by four stories of windows. The building contains three residential colleges with a combined total of 39 residential houses. On a warm, sunny day the green is full of students playing Frisbee, reading, and socializing. It is a huge living space.

The location is also noteworthy in another minor way. Behind the Quad are the science buildings and the Schools of Medicine and Veterinary Medicine; but in front of the building along Spruce Street are a collection of food trucks that offer meals that are reliable, quick, and inexpensive.

As I continued along Locust Walk, however, I came to another culinary locale: The Class of 1920 Commons. This giant dining hall – like most Ivy League dining locations – offers an impressive collection of food. Imagine people from around the world with varying restrictions, observances, and tastes. Vegans and paleos alike need to eat at Penn, and they can all find multiple options at the Commons.

I had a date with crepes, however, so I zipped by the Commons and across the 38th Street Bridge.

To my left was Huntsman Hall, the then-newly opened home of the Wharton School – the undergraduate and graduate school of business. The red stone building with its nine-story round tower is the biggest academic building at Penn with more than 320,000 square feet. It offers dozens of classrooms and study rooms, along with a handsome atrium of light wood and comfortable chairs.

Wharton is especially interesting to me because its brand may be more well-known and prestigious than the rest of the University of Pennsylvania. In terms of a business school, perhaps the Harvard Business School has more name recognition than Wharton, but the former relies on the strength of its host institution's name. Wharton stands alone as a brand.

On the far side of the bridge, Locust Walk turns to brick and runs under the trees, slicing between classroom and administrative buildings. Walking through this section of campus, I could spot several of my favorite iconic art pieces.

The first I came to was the statue of Benjamin Franklin. Most Ivies have one statue that draws tourists eager to appear in a picture. For Penn, this is the one. The effigy features a very life-like image of Ben Franklin, one arm resting on a walking stick, the other holding an edition of *The Pennsylvania Gazette*. Standing on the back of the bench is an equally life-like statue of a pigeon.

At the terminus of Locust Walk, I could see two semi-related art pieces. To the right towards College Hall sits a statue of a young Ben Franklin. The statue, built in 1899, depicts Franklin before his rise to fame. What this version of Ben lacked in wealth he made up for in girth. So pudgy was he, according to the story, that the bottom button on his vest – clearly missing on the statue – popped off and rolled across the plaza towards the Van Pelt Library. And that is where I could see the other piece in this collection: *The Split Button*. This 16-foot diameter, four-hole, white button is a modern art sculpture that has been at Penn since 1981.

I cut towards College Hall, passing by yet another piece of art: The Love Statue. The three-dimensional red letters – with the L and O over the V and E, and with the O askew in its orientation – are part of a larger art collection distributed around the country. It struck me as a sign of Penn's significance to serve as a backdrop to this piece of popular art.

I met Gretchen in Houston Hall and instantly felt at ease meeting someone with whom I shared a mutual contact. We grabbed our crepes and sat in front of a fireplace to eat and chat. We talked for a few minutes about Linda and Yale, comparing notes. I told her about my project and about my experiences at Penn so far.

She did not seem especially surprised about the experiences I had at Penn. "This is a weird place," she confided. "It's cliquey. You find your group and you stick with them. There's a lot of self-segregation."

I asked her about the term "social Ivy." I had heard Penn called the social Ivy often – but only by Penn students – and I frankly wasn't sure what it meant in the context of my relative isolation and Gretchen's comments.

"I'll tell you what," she said, pulling out her laptop. "I have some ideas to get you started. One of the coolest classes by one of the coolest professors is on mythology." She looked up the time of the class meetings. "I'll let the professor know that you will sit in on one. And American Foreign Policy meets right after that." She tapped out another e-mail to a professor. "How about the Vagina Monologues – have you seen it?" I hadn't. "I know someone involved in putting on a performance during Women's' Week. I'll introduce you to her and you can check out the show. Now for meeting students..." She quickly composed a brief message. She sent it to a list of contacts, and within seconds received a response. She chewed on her lip as she said, "Melanie and Sue want to meet with you for lunch tomorrow. Cool?"

It really, really was.

"They may not be the best people to talk to you about Penn," she added thoughtfully, "but it is a starting point."

So grateful was I for Gretchen's help as I walked away that I probably would not have even minded a parking ticket at my broken meter. The fact that I had managed to earn *two* tickets put only a slight damper on my mood.

*

One of my favorite parts of this silly project was that it afforded me an opportunity to indulge in one of my favorite activities: Attending classes. I enjoy listening to lectures or discussions by intelligent people on esoteric topics that leave me a bit smarter or more knowledgeable than I was when I walked in. The best parts are when they manage to be funny or entertaining in the process of educating me.

132

The Mythology class was a high-point in my travels throughout the Ivy League. The classroom itself was beautiful, with large windows veined with stone, cream colored pillars, and dark wood ceiling beams. The room was wired as a smart classroom with the latest in technology. The professor was young and amiable, with mannerisms that bespoke of humility. He wandered in and out of the classroom before he began teaching, and he continued to wander in front of his 200 pupils as he taught.

He began with Freud's assertion that myths dramatize the individual's psychological development. He talked about dreams as a socially acceptable valve through which to release the pent up steam of repression. According to Freud, myths were the dreams of an entire culture.

Despite his age – or perhaps through a charming affectation – the professor's attempts at pop culture references failed, resulting in the amusement of the class. In talking about dreams and repression, for instance, the professor said, "You don't dream about sleeping with your dad. Instead, he turns into Richard Hasselhoff."

He conducted a further exercise on the topic of repression. "Shhh...everyone clear your minds. Quiet, quiet. Think no thoughts." The room grew silent at his bidding. "Now: Picture your parents having sex!"

The class was a pleasant mix of furious note taking, quick thinking, and laughter.

The students were not just passive observers. The professor called for answers and input, and the room full of 20-year-olds rose to the occasion. At more than one point, a student raised a fact or issue that caused the professor to thoughtfully mutter, "Interesting..." sending him on a tangent. On one such divergent track, the professor engaged the technology in the room, dropping the blinds and lowering a screen on which he displayed a *New Yorker* cartoon labeled, "The Cosmology of Timmy."

133

The organizational chart listed God in the top space, and the first subordinate rung housed Santa Claus and the Tooth Fairy as a couple on the left, and a witch and the boogeyman on the right.

The conversation turned to Greek mythology, and the professor asked, "Why was Aphrodite born out of foam? What foam? Can anyone tell us the story?" He awkwardly explained, "I actually get a little embarrassed telling it." A hand went up and he cheerily declared, "Oh good – a volunteer!" He walked over to the undergrad, removing his lapel mike and handing it to her.

One of my favorite Penn moments occurred in this class – and again in the American Foreign Policy class that followed – when a group of students ran into the room in the middle of the professor's lecture. "I apologize for the interruption, professor, but we have a special valentine for Caitlin."

It was February 14, and the Glee Club was popping into classrooms to deliver singing telegrams as a part of a fundraiser.

"Please come in!" the prof insisted. "How long will it take?"

"Two minutes," said one of the students.

"That's too long. Can you do it in 30 seconds?"

The students looked at each other. "Yes."

"Go!"

They went and they delivered. It was only 30 seconds, but it was sweet and upbeat, with a song turning around the name Caitlin. When it ended, the class applauded loudly and the Glee Club quickly backed out of the auditorium on their way to their next appointment.

"Who was that for?" wondered the professor aloud. Nervous giggling, but no one raised a hand. "I won't make you stand up, but now everyone knows your name. Don't be mad at me – I didn't do it. Blame your valentine."

A 60-second diversion and then we were back to Freud and mythology.

*

Gretchen was right about the class, but she was also right about Melanie and Sue.

I met them in the café at Williams Hall. They had preceded me to the meeting and had picked a table in the middle of the room. It was a pretty busy time of day, and the tables around us were all occupied.

The two girls were pretty with dark hair and eyes. They were dressed fashionably – so much so that my first comment was to compliment Sue on her boots.

"You like them?" she asked rhetorically. "My mom just sent them from Florence. I think they are hideous, but they are expensive and Italian so I'll wear them."

"It could be worse," said Melanie, gesturing with her head towards the window. "Check them out."

Outside were two young girls walking by. They were wearing high heels – very, very high heels – that caused them to flail their arms slightly as they fought for balance. My lunch companions laughed openly at a sight that struck me as mildly sad.

"You should know that we are very fashion conscious at Penn," confided Melanie. "It takes a lot of money to fit in here."

"Money *and* work," Sue corrected.

"Tell me about the 'work' it takes," I suggested.

"Well, it isn't just that we are fashion conscious," she said. "We are more like appearance conscious. Everyone has to work out a lot to stay in shape. I'm used to it. I come from a wealthy town. We have like 10-year olds working out. My mom has six-pack abs. I'm the first to say that I am over privileged, but I blame my parents. It's just the way I was raised, but at least I fit in well here."

When someone begins to talk about the work it takes to attend an Ivy League school, a conversation about abdominal muscles is not where I imagine we are going.

135

Melanie jumped back in. "Yeah, physical beauty is important, but it comes back to money. It would be hard to go here if you don't have a lot of money. Especially for a boy. You need to buy lots of drinks and go to lots of nice restaurants if you want to date. And there is pressure to have the best spring break trips."

"Remember Luke?" Sue asked Melanie. "I heard he was on financial aid." She said it like it was a story about Luke's flatulence.

"So," I began, aiming for a subject change, "What do you do when you aren't in class?"

"You mean are we in a sorority?" That wasn't specifically where I was going, but I nodded. "Do we look like sorority girls?" asked Sue.

In fact, they did seem very much like sorority girls – on television. The sorority women I had met along the way impressed me with their abilities to undermine the popular stereotype. But these two girls were superficial and superficially attractive, as well as nasty and judgmental.

Not just judgmental, but proudly judgmental. Within seconds of acknowledging that they were in the same sorority, they brought up the rush process wherein new recruits are brought in. "I love rush. I love judging people," said Sue, and they went on to explain how a person's looks play a significant role in which sorority they enter.

Maybe they became aware of the distain that I was trying to suppress, because they became a bit defensive. "At least we're not discriminating," whined Melanie. "Our sorority admits both Christians and Jews. Some places don't."

"Yeah," added Sue. "What does Doug say about his fraternity? Their colors are green and white, because that is what you have to have and that is what you have to be to get in. We don't think like that."

"So you have black members, then?" I questioned.

The girls looked at each other. "Well, no. But not because they're African-Americans."

"Right," Sue said. "The black girls who rushed us just weren't very attractive. And we had an Asian member, I think."

They went on to explain that the apparent exclusion was not their doing. Penn, according to them, was self-segregating. People chose people like themselves – "We're kind of the same person," said one of the girls about the other – and they stuck together in social circles.

As they talked, I became aware that the people around us were listening in on our conversation. Students at nearby tables were reacting as the girls at my table spoke. I saw indignation and anger on many faces, accompanied by smirks and eye rolls.

My companions seemed oblivious.

Eventually, we were able to end our meeting and I slipped away quickly but temporarily. Once they were clear of the room, I went back to the café and sat with a young woman I recognized from a Qur'an course I was attending. She was one of the more notorious eye rollers.

I asked, "So how much of that could you hear?"

"Most of it," she responded. "I hope you don't hire them after that!"

"Hire them?" It turned out that she and a few of the other students who drifted over and joined us thought they were witnessing a job interview.

I explained my project about examining life in the Ivy League, and I asked for opinions on our conversation.

"The sad part is that they were right about most of it," said my classmate. "This place does have lots of segregation among student groups. We all do it to ourselves, but it's there."

"And they were right about the money," admitted a male student. "Look around. Students go out dressed to the nines for a morning class. It's all about labels and brand names – not about substance."

137

Another classmate disagreed. "That may be how it looks, but some of those students are Wharton students dressed for business classes or internships."

Nonetheless, self-segregation between the cliques and an obsession with appearance dominated many of the conversations that I had at Penn.

*

Penn did not work out the way I had planned. In many instances, I came close to a meaningful experience only to miss it.

I followed Gretchen's advice and connected with her friend, Hannah, who was one of the producers of the Vagina Monologues. Hannah was excited about my project as we spoke on Locust Walk during the ticket sale. I bought a ticket for the show, and Hannah arranged for me to come and watch a rehearsal.

But when I went to the rehearsal, I was rudely and summarily turned away by another student. It was a closed rehearsal, said she, not hearing my story of being invited by the producer as she physically pushed me out the door.

As I spoke with Hannah earlier that day, however, she introduced me to another undergraduate – an actress in the show. She was part of a popular sorority, and they were planning an evening of storytelling and comradery. Some of my best moments at Dartmouth were spent similarly, as the only male witnessing a private event in a sorority. I was thrilled when Gretchen's friend invited me to attend.

And I was crushed when she withdrew the invitation an hour later via email. She expressed a concern that my presence would be disruptive to the environment of sisterhood. Hard to argue against that.

It wasn't until the end of my time that I began to make connections with students who were more dependable, relatable, and eager to discuss Penn.

On a rainy day, I took a tour with Todd. Todd was an officer in one of the fraternities, and he seemed destined for political greatness. In a 10-minute walk, he must have delivered two dozen handshakes to men and at least as many kisses to women. He was warm and smiling, with something nice to say about everyone – to their faces and behind their backs. "Here is one of the best guys I know," he said as we were approached by a male classmate. "Here's my valentine!" he said of multiple women. He was hailed by an older woman passing by, whom he kissed before introducing me to "one of the best professors at Penn!" People seemed excited to see him, and he seemed genuinely glad for every connection.

He showed me through his fraternity house as we talked about segregation. He agreed with many of the comments I had heard – that students tended to cluster into cliques and that one deciding factor was often a matter of money – but he was disappointed that I had not been introduced to more of those cliques. He stated that if we had met earlier, he could have accomplished that. Indeed, between our walk across campus, our tour of the fraternity house, and a trip to the impressive gym on Walnut Street, he had introduced me to students of all colors, creeds, and majors.

"You should come back," he suggested.

I started to protest, but the words stuck in my throat. I was off to Columbia University next, but they would be leaving for spring break at the end of my time there. How much could I observe during a break?

As I thought about it, Todd persisted. "I know this trip wasn't the greatest, but give it another shot. I love Penn and I want you to see the social Ivy the way it should be. I know someone at the *Daily Pennsylvanian*. We'll let the students know that you'll be back, and then let us show you around!"

I knew that my story would be subjective – a tale of my adventures – so I did not need to seek balance or equity in my story. To that end, I felt that I should just allow the action to ensue without trying too hard to overtly manipulate the outcome. In other words, there was value to a disappointing chapter.

But – perhaps as an alumnus or as a college fan – I did not want to leave the record as it was. If I had an opportunity to gather more stories, I could not easily pass on it under these circumstances.

I agreed with Todd that I would return. We set a date and I walked to my car. I removed the parking ticket from under my windshield wiper, hopped in, and headed to New York City.

COLUMBIA UNIVERSITY IN THE CITY OF NEW YORK

Q: How many Columbia students does it take to change a light bulb?

A: Seventy-six – One to change the light bulb, fifty to protest the light bulb's right to not change, and twenty-five to hold a counter protest.

Columbia was founded in 1754 under the name King's College. Today, it sports the longest name in the Ivy League: Columbia University in the City of New York. Only a crazy person would use the full name in casual conversation, and on all but formal occasions, the school is called "Columbia" or "Columbia University."

It is fitting, however, that the official name includes the City of New York. I suppose to some extent location defines each Ivy. Cornell residing in the art community of Ithaca; Yale sitting in stark contrast to New Haven; and Princeton appropriately located in and named after Princeton, New Jersey. But somehow Columbia is *more* about its location. The school is in NYC, and there is no escaping that fact.

The reputation of the school is defined by student activism. The school was at the center of a protest that received international media coverage in 1968. The students were protesting the university's affiliation with the Institute for Defense Analyses – a Department of Defense research lab conceiving new weapon systems – and the proposed construction of a new gym in Morningside Park. The students barricaded themselves in major university buildings, and the New York Police Department was brought in to break up the protest.

In the end, the students won. The university broke its ties with the Pentagon, and they found a new location for the gym. The protest crippled the school temporarily, and it continues to be a major part of Columbia lore.

I arrived in February very much aware of the reputation for student activism and outspokenness on issues. I harbored a little concern in this area. Among the many issues on which Columbia students are known to have strong opinions is the military. Shortly after the Institute for Defense Analyses debacle, Columbia kicked ROTC off of the campus in protest of the Vietnam War. I was mindful of the fact that while Columbia students were holding these protests, my father was in Vietnam. ROTC continued to be disallowed from Columbia throughout the conflicts I brushed up against during my military service. Furthermore, at the time of my visit, ROTC had not been allowed to return to campus; and my little brother, Jason, was still serving on active duty.

If I could learn about the community's feelings about the military while on campus, great; but I was not dispassionate on that particular issue, and I hoped it would not distract from my goal of exploring Columbia University.

*

One of my biggest concerns as I started this project was where I would live in New York. While I could stay with students occasionally, I needed a dependable place to go to in a pinch. Hotels did the trick in many places, but a semi-decent hotel in the city would cost over $200 per night.

Fortunately, it didn't come to that.

Katie, my old law school buddy who was so much fun at Brown, insisted that I stay with her. She was working in Manhattan, but she lived on the third floor of a brownstone walk-up in the Park Slope neighborhood of Brooklyn. She had an extra room for me and gave me a key so I could come and go.

It was almost a perfect situation. There were only two negative points:

142

1. The only toilet, she said, was extremely sensitive – so sensitive that it could not manage anything that was not in liquid form. (I would advise you to not overthink it.)
2. Park Slope is a long way from Morningside Heights where Columbia is located.

The trip from Katie's place to Columbia was an adventure. I boarded the Q train on Flatbush Avenue and headed across the East River to intersect with the 3 line. One more switch to the 1-9 line and I was heading uptown in Manhattan. Once on that train, it was a straight but long shot to the stop at 116th Street. The subways were tedious, but the people watching was entertaining, and the subways generally felt clean and safe enough.

I climbed the stairs at the subway station and emerged on Broadway. It was the same Broadway associated with the theater, but at a point far from the theater district. The upper west side of New York was thoroughly urban. Restaurants and shops lined the streets which were clogged with cars, buses, and taxis – issuing a steady stream of exhaust visible in the cold air and occasionally sounding a horn in frustration, warning, or encouragement. People bustled up the wide sidewalks, dressed for winter and keeping to themselves.

At the top of the subway stop, it was only a matter of steps before I passed through the gates and found myself on campus at Columbia University. The city was behind me; and the Ivy League campus was before me.

Columbia's campus has served as a backdrop to many movies, making it a familiar sight even for first-time visitors. The first two *Spiderman* movies starring Tobey Maguire and Kirsten Dunst were relatively fresh in the popular culture at the time of my visit. Not only was Peter Parker sadistically attacked by a radioactive spider on campus in the first movie, but Peter was a student at

143

Columbia by the second movie. In fact, Peter took a course in 309 Havermeyer Hall – one of the most filmed classrooms in the world, owing in part to its location in New York City and in part to the fact that it *looks* like a classroom with plenty of seats arranged in a semicircle on two tiers.

The view from College Walk was also a part of the 1980s classic *Ghostbusters* movies. The three original ghostbusters worked at Columbia – not so named in the movie – before they were given the boot. Interestingly, the *Ghostbuster* movies typically sprang to my mind as I trekked up the Walk – not because the Low Library where many scenes were shot was on my left, but because of the green space on my right. The rumor around campus was that the landscaping and the green were maintained through *Ghostbuster* money.

Of course, my visit was in February, and in my first days on campus, New York received over seven inches of snow. So the green was thoroughly buried for most of my time on campus during the project.

This particular visit, however, did not represent most of my time on campus. I visited Columbia while I considered attending its Law School, but I had also studied at Columbia for one term as a graduate student. I was not a learner on campus long enough for it to feel like home – I was discovering in my travels that urban-centered campuses were not my personal preference – but it was at least familiar. Moreover, I still had a recent Columbia student ID card and a functioning Columbia e-mail address. Thus, I was able to navigate Columbia with more ease than some places.

The navigating that I did usually took me straight to the Low Memorial Library. Again, the building is movie-famous, but it is also Ivy-League-famous. The white granite building with its 10 pillars resembles the Pantheon in Rome, but it sits under a domed roof that is not easily mistaken.

My favorite part of the building is the steps that ascend from the plaza below to the doors above. The steps are a reliable staging point for protesting students, and there is often activity afoot. With the massive snowfall, I discovered a steep sled-riding course in place of the steps. Columbia students sat on food trays from the dining halls and braved the steep, snowy descent.

Another interesting bit of trivia about the steps is that they are not uniform in depth. The steps get steeper and harder to ascend the higher up you climb. At first, I thought it might be my imagination or the winter taking a toll on my health. I discovered, however, that the steps were designed that way with a specific intent: To create a physical barrier between the scholars at Columbia who needed to use the library and the non-academic folk who might walk by. It seemed to me an interesting concept as I watched those revered geniuses – some in ski garb and some in beach clothes – catapulting themselves down the stairs on food trays.

But the best part of the stairs is the *Alma Mater* sculpture. This statue depicts the Greek goddess Athena upon a throne, with a scepter in one hand, the other hand open and upturned, and a book across her lap. The sculpture sits on the steps welcoming the Columbia community – and marking the line behind which the stairs really start to work your glutes. The statue is a symbol of the university and was a target for domestic terrorists in the 1960s. Hidden on the statue – I won't say where – is a carving of an owl. The legend is that the first person in each freshman class to find it will become the class valedictorian. Good luck!

I would be remiss if I did not mention that while the *Alma Mater* is my favorite piece of outdoor artwork for its complexity, my close second favorite is *Curl*. It is a large metal sculpture created by the minimalist artist Clement Meadmore. The artwork appears to change shape as it is viewed from different angles. My favorite story is that this piece sits in front of the Columbia Business School in Uris Hall – the place to go to earn a high-paying job – and when it is viewed from the top of Uris, the *Curl* sculpture appears to be a large dollar sign.

Low has been known to confuse a few people. Despite the fact that the inscription, "The library of Columbia University" is carved deeply into the white granite over the door, and despite the fact that the edifice is called the "Low Memorial Library," the building is *not* a library. It served in this capacity between its construction in 1895 and the construction of the bigger Butler Library in 1934. At the time of my visit, it served as an administration building housing the office of the president, among others. Due to the fact that the books and archives have been relocated, and due to the fact that it sits high atop the steps, students will occasionally remark that the building is neither low nor a library.

From the stairs of Low, I could see the Butler Library crouching across the green (or white) space on campus. Butler seemed to be designed with Low in mind, matching in some respects – a rare quality on an Ivy League campus – with white granite, many pillars, and a weathered, green roof. The names carved into the exterior of the library served to inspire me: Homer, Plato, Demosthenes, Aquinas, Dante, and Voltaire.

On my first day on campus, I defied subways, snow, and steps. I visited the *Alma Mater* on the steps of Low and found the owl. I considered for a second taking a turn on a tray flying at 80 miles per hour down the steps. At 34, I always felt starkly out of place among my 21-year old contacts, and I figured that a broken hip was not going to make me feel any better about this.

*

All of the Ivies have academic units embedded within them, and Columbia has many schools under its umbrella. It has schools of law, business, medicine, and journalism, but it has other, more complex relationships. For example, Columbia is affiliated with Teachers College – a unit with its own president, but which also serves as a department within the larger University. Furthermore, the University offers joint undergraduate programs with the Jewish Theological Seminary of America and the Juilliard School. The relationships between academic units were more complicated and numerous than I encountered at any other school.

My exploration of Columbia revolved around four of these units: Columbia College, the School of Engineering and Applied Sciences, the School of General Studies, and Barnard College.

My first meetings on campus were with undergraduates at Columbia College. These were students studying the arts and sciences in the heart of this Ivy League institution. This college can trace its roots all the way back to 1754 and is the oldest part of the University.

It was from this group of scholars that I developed an appreciation for the word "hum." When used by a Columbia College student, the word is most often a shortcut for "Humanities." To graduate, all undergraduate students must have exposure to a wide variety of subjects, and they get this exposure through taking core courses, many of which include the word "Humanities." Thus, it is not unusual to overhear such nuggets as, "I love music hum," or "What time do you have lit hum?" The courses in the core were notorious for being exceptionally interesting with great instructors.

The students in the College were what I tend to imagine when I imagine an Ivy League student. I met people who had studied abroad along with approximately 25% of their classmates; I encountered students who worked for the Vice President of the United States; and I met undergrads who were recognized professional actors.

147

The students in the Fu Foundation School of Engineering and Applied Sciences, or SEAS (pronounced "seize"), are different from other undergrads at Columbia, according to their academic peers. The difference can be summed up succinctly: SEAS students have a reputation for being smarter. Columbia's engineering school is at the top of the intellectual food chain in the Ivy League, second in the world only to the Massachusetts Institute of Technology.

And, for what it's worth, SEAS has a fantastic coat of arms. Columbia University has a seal of royal blue with a light blue chevron and three white crowns. The SEAS logo employs one of the crowns from the university seal, and it adds crossed hammers behind it. It bespeaks of the history of an Ivy League school with some badass tools.

SEAS is smaller than the College, but with the academic street cred the engineers have, its students are not thought of as lesser-than.

The School of General Studies, on the other hand, has an inferiority complex. Its mission, paraphrased, is to provide a high-quality, Ivy League education to non-traditional and returning students. A Columbia College undergrad who stops out for more than a year must finish through General Studies. Adult and military students typically enter through this unit where the average age of learners is 28. Students who attend from outside of the city can apply for housing at Columbia, they enroll in the same courses as other Columbia undergrads, and their degree is the same as those of their peers in Columbia College and SEAS.

Students who were not in General Studies typically spoke of the school as a "backdoor" into Columbia. If a person lacked the academic fortitude to earn admission to the College, the School of General Studies might be a pathway in. I understood the sentiment, but it did not seem to be quite accurate. The School of General Studies is selective – it is not easy to earn admission – and the school serves a different audience. Comparisons between this group and others seem unfair.

I was especially interested to learn what General Studies students thought of themselves and others. I had met several students individually – most notably, Mark, who was a veteran and willing to orient me to the school – but I was hoping to see a collection of General Studies students together. The problem was that they tended not to cluster; they were dispersed throughout the institution of Columbia.

Mark pointed me towards a brunch for his colleagues in the school, so I made my way via subway to the university on a Sunday. I entered the GS Lounge in Lewisohn Hall ready to learn about the School of General Studies. What I found was a disparate group of about 15 undergraduates, most of whom were sitting uncomfortably by themselves not talking. Mark was not there, and I knew no one. The students seemed much younger than I had expected, and the atmosphere was not conducive to me polling the group.

With a sigh, I turned to the other thing I found there: Bagels and lox. It was not especially helpful in my pursuit of this project, but Columbia does breakfast better than any other school I visited. Years later, images of Columbia spring to mind every time I encounter salmon at breakfast time.

It was the fourth undergraduate unit – Barnard College – that was most intriguing to me.

The Ivy League schools are an interesting case study in the treatment of women in higher education. In the case of Cornell, women were admitted directly to the University from its inception. At Yale, women were not admitted as undergraduates until the policy changed in 1969. Brown had the women's college at Pembroke that was eventually merged and dismantled.

Barnard is a women's college. It has the things you would imagine a college to have: A campus, a faculty, a

149

history department, a president, dormitories, etc. To get into Barnard, one must apply to Barnard; when one graduates, the diploma is from Barnard.

And it is from Columbia University.

A history major at Barnard will almost certainly take classes at Barnard and at Columbia. A history major at Columbia is just as welcome to take classes at Barnard. The two campuses are just across Broadway from each other, and students comingle on a regular basis. Barnard and Columbia are decidedly independent entities that are closely aligned and cooperative.

Just as with General Studies, I heard many Columbia College students talk about Barnard as a backdoor to Columbia University. Sitting with a group of young men and women in the Café 212 in Learner Hall, I broached the subject of Barnard. The reaction was swift.

"Barnard students are *not* Columbia students," insisted a woman named Geri. "I remember overhearing a girl from Barnard talking to someone and she said, 'I am a Columbia student.' I was like, 'Wait, no you're not!'"

Her friend, Leroy, jumped in. "They use Barnard as a way of getting into Columbia. Barnard is the number one source of transfer applications for Columbia."

"Hold on," I said, confused. "You mean that students at Barnard formally apply to come over to Columbia?" Nods all around. "Why?"

"Well, because they want to be *real* Columbia students."

"Why don't they just apply as freshmen?" I asked.

"Some do," stated the third member of the trio, Susan. "We can apply to both at the same time. Some students are admitted to Barnard and not admitted to Columbia. Those are the ones who want to transfer. Sometimes they are admitted to both."

"The people who are happy at Barnard are typically those who would not be happy at Columbia," said Leroy. "Barnard students have different values. They want to celebrate women-hood. Not that there is anything wrong with that," he added hastily, "but at Columbia it is more about people than gender."

"Yeah," Susan said, "the saying is that Barnard girls dress to impress men and Columbia girls dress to impress women. The Barnard girls have a reputation of being slutty. You can always pick them out in a bar."

"Or they're gay," from Leroy. "You can probably pick them out in a gay bar."

I found it hard to believe that those were the only two options, so I set out to speak with Barnard students.

I met with my first two Barnard undergrads, appropriately, in Barnard Hall. It is a beautiful building of dark red brick with white limestone accents set behind a black, wrought iron gate. I met with Ashley and Robin in a comfortable sitting area, opened my notebook to the pages about the meeting with the Columbia College students, and attempted to cover the same ground.

"It's true that we could apply to both Columbia and Barnard," acknowledged Ashley. "I know several people who did that. But I only know of one case where someone was admitted to Barnard but not Columbia."

Robin was nodding along. "Almost every time I've heard of someone applying to both, they were either admitted to both or rejected from both."

"If they are admitted to both, do they always choose Columbia?" I inquired.

"No," Ashley responded. "I know two people in our year that got into both and chose Barnard."

"But more choose Columbia, I think," admitted Robin. "But that is about admissions. As far as transferring, I don't think it is a mass exodus."

Ashley supported her. "Maybe it's happening, but the majority of the students I know are very happy at Barnard, and those who aren't happy wouldn't be happier at Columbia."

"And why wouldn't they be happier?" I probed, attempting to angle into the areas of sluttiness and lesbianism.

Not unexpectedly, that isn't where these two women went. They described how supportive the community was. They told me about the opportunities and options that they had as Barnard students. They commented on how they had everything they could have at Columbia and then some.

"Is sexual orientation a big factor here?" I asked awkwardly.

"Do you mean, are we all dykes?" responded Robin. She suddenly looked very beefy and very angry. Her muscles seemed to be flexing under her athletic sweatshirt.

"Err...kinda."

"No," she said without a smile.

Fortunately for me, Ashley was more gracious and articulate in the face of my obnoxious question. "There are a lot of lesbians here," she said, "but there are a lot of lesbians in Columbia College, too. This is a very gay-friendly environment, and I guess there are a lot of lesbians, but it isn't a big deal. I don't think I know anyone who is here because of that."

"In fact," added Robin, recovering from my question, "if we're known for anything involving sex, it isn't lesbianism."

"Really?" I wondered. "What is it?"

"Barnard students are known to be slutty," she replied gruffly.

"Yep," said Ashley, "you can always pick the Barnard students out at the bar."

As strange as it sounded coming from non-Barnard people, it sounded even stranger coming from genuine Barnard students. I heard this same sentiment from other undergrads across the universe of Columbia. It struck me as not especially healthy, but so pervasive that it would be a glaring omission if I were to ignore it.

My firsthand observations of Barnard women left me with a great impression of them. I spent quite a bit of time on the west side of Broadway. I socialized with Ashley, Robin, and other Barnard students. I attended classes in Lehman and Altschul Halls. I especially enjoyed my time with the theater and music communities at Barnard. The students I met were scholarly and practical – comfortable with theory, but worldlier than some I had met along the way.

The undergrads of Columbia University identified one common theme that seemed to transcend any differences between the schools: They believed they possessed maturity and independence in greater measures than their Ivy League comrades at other schools.

Certainly New York City is a harsh backdrop for a university. The city has a reputation as a tough place – definitely not a place for the weak. It fosters an attitude of sink or swim among its residents. Take a group of young college kids, away from home for the first time in many cases, and drop them in this environment. They certainly are not on their own – the university provides support and care for its students – but they are still residents of a concrete jungle.

They may have drawn lines between themselves, but they were an impressive group collectively.

*

While I was conducting my examination into the lives of people at the Ivy League universities, I also had occasion to explore another exclusive lifestyle.

Katie provided me with more than a place to call home base in New York City. She was living a life that I might have lived. She graduated from an Ivy League law school and took a job at a large and prestigious law firm on Wall Street. (It strikes me as interesting that Wall Street is often a metonym for finance and banking, but in this case Katie worked on *the* Wall Street.) Just a year out of school, she could see a clear path to salaries of almost half a million dollars a year while working in an honored and exclusive profession. Living with her, I was able to see what my life could have been like had I been more traditional.

The first thing I noticed was that Katie was absent. She headed to work each weekday morning before 9 a.m. On a normal weekday, she arrived home in a town car around 2 a.m., at which point she would fall into bed. Saturdays she was more kind to herself, going in around 10 a.m. and returning around 7 p.m. She chose to go into work only every other Sunday, giving herself a couple of days off each month.

When we did bump into each other around the apartment, she was not enthusiastic about her work. Law is a traditional profession where newbies pay their dues before being entrusted with tasks such as going to court, participating in meetings, or speaking when not spoken to. We never discussed the substance of her work, but it seemed to lack entertainment or color. "It ain't *Law & Order*," she assured me.

That is not to say that it was without drama. That clear path to riches and rewards could be blocked by a single ornery partner or senior associate. The trick was to offend no one. The problem is that it was often unclear what would cause offense. Some people hated tardiness; others viewed promptness as a statement that the associate was underworked. Some partners wanted associates who could think and argue; many wanted underlings who were meek and obedient. Katie was spending about 100 hours each week in a minefield.

When you add this professional anxiety to the fact that Katie maintained a suspicion that I would ignore her warnings and attempt to flush a bowl of Fruit Loops down her toilet, you can appreciate the toll that life was taking on my friend.

As much as I admired Katie for her dedication, I was secretly glad for the bizarre life I had made for myself. It was one thing to bounce from campus to campus worrying about where I would sleep; it was another to have my own comfortable bed in an apartment I rarely visited.

*

One of the main dining facilities that I visited at Columbia was John Jay Dining Hall. It was as good as any campus-sponsored place that I ate along the way – with as much choice, health, and decadence as any other – but it was friendlier than most I saw.

At first, I thought it was a factor of the students that I joined for lunch. When Harvey approached the grille and the woman working behind it, he loudly called, "Hello, Wilma!" The woman smiled broadly and returned the greeting. At the check-out line, Louis introduced me to Iris, the woman ringing up our order. Walking to our table, we encountered the manager who stopped to say hello to the three of us.

Sitting down, Harvey and Louis told me that the staff in the dining hall was on a first name basis with most undergrads. As for Wilma, she strictly enforced her rule that students must say hello to her if they wanted her to serve them. The students advised me that even on a stressful day, they looked forward to seeing the dining hall staff. In a city not exactly known for its warm embrace of people, the dining facility at John Jay did what it could to compensate.

I did not, however, spend much time eating on campus.

On one of my very first days there, I went to Koronet Pizza on the advice of students. The restaurant was not big – in typical New York fashion – but the pizzas were –

also in typical New York fashion. A single slice was almost enough for me, and it was less than four dollars a slice. But the best part was that the person who served me had an accent. It was easy to find a Puerto Rican or an Indian accent in a pizza place in the city, but this guy actually had an Italian accent. As he handed me my slice, he assured me, "You're a-gonna like it!" And he was right.

I also could not help but visit Tom's Restaurant at the corner of Broadway and West 112th Street. The fact that it was the inspiration for Suzanne Vega's song "Tom's Diner" was lost on me – and for those of you who now have the tune stuck in your heads, I sincerely apologize – but the exterior of the restaurant was the image used in the television series *Seinfeld* for the diner where the characters used to eat.

Once I mastered the eateries of Columbia, I was determined to explore where people lived.

Living in New York City is always awe inspiring for me. A space for which I might pay $500 per month in my hometown could cost $5,000 per month in the city. I knew people who had bought their 700 square-foot fourth floor walk-up apartments in Manhattan for a seven-figure sum. How could Columbia students afford to live?

Like most schools, Columbia had residence halls. I spent a day and a night in the "social dorm" at Carman Hall; and I spent less time in other, allegedly less fun dorms. The buildings themselves were disappointingly uninteresting. The walls were exposed cinder block for the most part, and the fanciest features were the occasional television room or pool table. Nothing like residence halls I experienced at other schools. Then again, the cities I had seen were nothing like New York.

The dorms were only half of the story anyway. The university's housing options included apartment buildings and brownstones in the area. Students could live near the campus under the security and predictability of Columbia, but be one step closer to life in the big city.

Columbia also had some Greek life. Fraternities and sororities made up a clear minority of students with fewer than 15% of undergraduates participating. Those who did participate, however, could find houses waiting for them on West 114th Street. I visited one fraternity house with a newly pledged freshman who assured me that he was not interested in moving in. "I'm looking forward to moving into a co-ed dorm. I can't wait," he confided. "I like girls too much to live in an all-male house."

Housing runs on a lottery system. The better your number, the earlier you get to choose and the more likely you are to end up where you want to be. Which made me wonder what happened if you ended up with the worst possible number – the number that won you the very last choice among the thousands of students?

I didn't meet this person, but I did meet the student with the *second worst* number in the lottery. He landed on his feet, finding a place on West 112th Street. The building was not owned by Columbia, but it was traditionally rented by Columbia community members.

The opportunity to attend a world-class research university is what would draw me first. Perhaps the allure of the City of New York is an equally big draw. Add on some giant slices of pizza and a place to sleep, and I am surprised that even more people don't flock to Columbia.

*

I am gullible.

When I see an ad in a newspaper that says, "Work at home and earn more than $3,000 per week!" I think, "Hey, I could do that!"

When I get a phone call from a person offering me a free vacation, I ask for more information.

And when someone from Columbia's Marching Band sent me an e-mail telling me that I should go and watch their group practice because, "Marching Band is sexy," I showed up.

I went to high school. I know what marching band is. I should have known better.

It was raining, so the huge band was crammed in a small, hot room that smelled like human stew. It was hard to judge the sexiness of the band, but how sexy can you be while operating a tuba? This was a scramble band – the first in the Ivy League – that was confined in a small space, so I am sure I missed their best that day. In any case, sexy is not the adjective that I would have chosen.

What the band might have lacked in cool they made up for with enthusiasm. Not every student played an instrument – which I found confusing, seeing as how they were a marching *band* – but those who did really played the heck out of them. *Zeal* is the word that springs to my mind when I think of them. It was a party atmosphere – although if it were a party, it might involve pointy hats and a piñata rather than beer and strippers.

For all of that, the Columbia University Marching Band was known for controversy and cleverness. They had produced shows that pantomimed the consummation of a same-sex marriage, the burning of an American flag, and the assassination of John F. Kennedy – not all at once, mind you, but still impressive. Only a couple of years before my visit, the band joked before a game against Fordham University that their tuition was "going down like an altar boy," leading to a ban on the Columbia band at Fordham games. I am all for freedom of speech, cleverness, and edginess. I began to warm to them despite myself.

Part of their humor came through just in their name. Their acronym was CUMB. In response to the question, "How do you pronounce it?" they responded that the B is silent, like in the word "bass." And part of their comradery came through in their policy that they would raise bail if any of their members were arrested – a policy that they claimed was occasionally tested.

I would be remiss if I did not mention the tradition of Orgo Night. The CUMB had a history of taking over the main reading room in Butler Library at one minute to midnight the night before an Organic Chemistry final exam. This was one of the most challenging courses at Columbia, often marking the divide between future medical doctors and people who could not handle the science to pursue medical degrees. As a result, Butler would be chock full of scholars cramming for this important test. The band's mission was to create an amusing disruption. The tradition was well-loved, with students of all sorts flooding the library to see what the band would do.

While I was not present for an Orgo Night, I did have another occasion to see the CUMB in action.

On a Saturday evening, I attended a women's basketball game against Yale. I went into the Dodge Physical Fitness Center. Dodge is located on the main campus – as opposed to the primary athletic campus far uptown at 218th Street – and it is a source of minor controversy.

Remember that one of the issues in the 1968 protest was the proposal of a new gymnasium – a state of the art structure designed to fit into Morningside Heights. The students felt that the new gym would encroach on Harlem and was an act of aggression against black residents of the area. The university ultimately sold the plans for the new gym to Princeton, and they built a substitute – and, I think it is fair to say, lesser – facility underground on the campus.

I entered that storied facility and found my way into the Levien Gymnasium. I sat in the impressively named Lions Den section of the bleachers with an unimpressive 20 other people. Yale's team had more supporters in the house than we had on the Columbia side, but we had a few advantages.

First, we had some of the most scantily-clad cheerleaders I had encountered. They were fiercely enthusiastic, and they made it difficult for me to avert my eyes.

Second, we were joined by a strange mascot. I was not clear exactly who he was at the time, but a large amphibian with green skin and impossibly red hair got the crowd riled up and then sat with me in the stands. J.J. Jumper, it turned out, was the mascot for the NCAA conference.

And, of course, we had the CUMB. They wore blue and white horizontally striped shirts; some also inexplicably wore orange vests. They played canned music, and occasionally played their instruments over it – rarely, it seemed, playing the same song. Everything they did, they did with a smile, and the diminutive crowd seemed to sincerely appreciate them.

There is much more to the band. For example, there is the matter of the initiation ritual. But some things must remain secret. If I told you, they would probably kill me. Or at least their half orc fighters would take several hit-points from my wizard.

*

I bumped into Ashley from Barnard walking to a class on a Friday morning. She told me that she was going out with a group of friends that night, and she wanted to invite me along. "It won't just be us, though," she warned. "It's a club, so we'll be there along with a bunch of our friends, but people from across the city will be there, too."

I knew that Ashley was a sophomore, and she seemed to be of traditional age – certainly not 21. "Err...will you be able to get in?"

She smiled, taking my meaning right away. "Well, I have a fake ID." She said it as if I were a bit dim. "We all have fake IDs. We buy them in our first terms."

I subsequently spoke with scores of Columbia students, male and female, who confirmed this phenomenon. The purchase of IDs seemed to be an organized affair, with upperclassmen assisting their naïve newbies. In fact, I was sitting in on a course in Hartley Hall when the class – pupils and professor – celebrated one student's birthday with chocolates. As the class discussed how lucky the new 21-year old was, one of his classmates mentioned, "I can't wait until I turn 21 next year . . . although I guess I'm 23 in New Jersey right now."

After Ashley ran off, I reached out to my housemate, Katie, to see if she wanted to join me. "Maybe, if it's late. I'm going to leave work early tonight – around nine o'clock." *Good grief.* "I'm meeting some of my friends for a costume party at nine-thirty. How about we come straight from that and meet you at eleven-thirty?"

That is how I found myself in strange company in a New York City nightclub. On one side, I had a group of Barnard women – who, by the way, I could not pick out in the bar. On my other side, I had an all-lesbian cast of the *Wizard of Oz.*

Katie was an attractive scarecrow with her sandy blonde hair and pieces of straw sticking out of her snazzy attorney suit. We had a tall tin man, a butch Dorothy, and even a woman dressed as Toto. We also had Chelsea – a heavy woman stuffed into a lion costume. She was three parts vodka, two parts annoying when I met her. Chelsea was excessively confident and convinced of her own virtues.

The college girls danced and danced, stopping occasionally to drink and socialize with us. I talked with them about life at Columbia in between dances. They told me about their adventures in dating and partying in New York. Over the course of the evening, more women and a

161

few men from their circle came over to talk to me. All the while, Chelsea hovered over one shoulder, correcting the students and insisting that Columbia had nothing on Hofstra University – her alma mater.

The girls often tried to drag me onto the dance floor. Sometimes it seemed perfunctory, but some of the women seemed intent on me having a good time. I begged off insisting that I dance like a walrus having a convulsion, but they persisted. "You can at least slow dance, right?" asked Ashley.

When I admitted that I could slow dance, the project shifted to finding me someone with whom to dance. Ashley and her friends began scoping the crowd for a suitable partner for me. Every time the girls discussed a prospective partner, Chelsea would announce loudly that their choice was a lesbian.

The girls eventually settled on a woman across the bar. She was indeed very pretty, carefully put together and flashing a wide smile. I began to feel the pressure of the group egging me on. They were confident that a slow song would be starting in a matter of seconds, so time was of the essence. In an effort to be a good sport, I obliged.

In retrospect, I should have seen the problem from a distance. It was not that the woman was attractive; it was that she was with several attractive friends. Women by themselves can be heartbreaking, but traveling in a pack, they can turn cruel. Like hyenas.

As the tempo and lighting in the club switched to romance, I approached the posse. "Hi," I said, showing what I hoped was a disarming smile. "Would you like to dance?"

The woman froze. I saw her friends watching her to see what she would do, and I saw her noticing her friends watching. She looked me up and down, and her lip curled into a sneer. "With you? No."

I was mortified. She seemed delighted with her response, and I could see appreciation of her ruthlessness in the eyes of her friends.

What I wish I had done was to say, "What? You misunderstand. I said, 'You look really fat in those pants.'"

Instead, I just turned and dashed back to my friends.

It was time to go. We were creeping up on 2 a.m., and my dignity had taken a serious hit. I offered my goodbyes to Ashley and her classmates, Katie rounded up her friends, and we hit the yellow brick road.

Outside, Chelsea remained confident. "I *told* you," she repeated. "I *told* you she was a lesbian. *I* should have asked her to dance. Then you would have seen."

The tin man and Toto tried to shush her, but she was persistent. "She would have been all over me. I saw her looking at me."

"And why do you think she was looking at you?" Katie asked, tiredly.

"Because I'm hot. She wanted some of *this*." To clarify the object of her demonstrative, Chelsea ran her hands over her lumpy midsection.

"What?" Katie said with sincere disbelief. "You are a heinous fat girl dressed as a cat. Be quiet."

Strangely, it worked. Chelsea was pleasantly quiet for the remainder of the night. I remain grateful to Katie for finding the off-switch.

*

I left Columbia pleasantly surprised.

I went in with my expectations sufficiently managed. After all, one semester as a graduate student was all I really needed, and I already knew that the city was a fine place to visit, but not for me long-term.

It was the students at Columbia who changed my mind. They were right about being independent. I met great people across the Ivy League, but my age stood as a barrier between me and them. I felt this less at Columbia. The undergrads were young, but they were not children.

As a matter of fact, as I prepared to leave, I realized one of the things that I liked most about Columbia students: They did not use the word "kids" to refer to themselves as often as their colleagues at other schools did. For me, I had a day when I was 18 where I thought of myself as a kid; the next day, I was in the military, and I never thought of myself as a kid again. It struck me as odd to the point of distraction to hear 20-year olds saying, "Me and a couple of other kids are going to class."

Two things I did not encounter at Columbia were a major protest or explicit anti-military sentiment. It may have been there, brewing beneath the surface – I suppose it is a side effect of independence that people have the urge to fight for their ideals – but it did not impact my visit.

My new friends were heading off on spring break. Some were returning to their homes around the country and the world. A few were heading to traditional destinations in Florida and Mexico. One was going to Utah to ski, another destined for Texas with Habitat for Humanity.

I was heading back to Philadelphia for another crack at the University of Pennsylvania.

THE UNIVERSITY OF PENNSYLVANIA - REVISITED

Q: How many Penn students does it take to change a light bulb the second time around?

A: Three – one to change it and two to make fun of his shoes while he does it.

In mid-March as the Columbia undergraduate students were heading out on spring break, I slipped back home to Pittsburgh, Pennsylvania. I had plenty of work left to do – and I was scheduled to revisit the University of Pennsylvania later in the week – but seeing everyone else going on break inspired me to do the same.

My first night home, Shawn Hogan took me to his favorite bar, Big Mike's. A few things you might like to know about Big Mike's:

1. While there is a Mike, he is about 5'5" and approximately 100 pounds. But he owns the bar, and he can call it anything he wants.
2. It is a local bar, but not exactly local to Shawn. It is about 40 minutes from his house. Why he goes on a road trip every time he wants to hang out, I don't know.
3. I am not a connoisseur of bars, but even I know this bar is a bit scary.

Nevertheless, to Big Mike's we went.

We were two of about 20 patrons, including two identifiable women and another close call. Most of the customers were sitting on bar stools or talking to people on bar stools, and everyone had at least one beer bottle in front of them. Shawn was better dressed than many of his peers, but he was boisterously welcomed, and he ordered a beer to keep up appearances.

I, on the other hand, was dressed in black dress pants and a sweater, and I ordered a glass of water. I was not exactly welcomed, but I was certainly closely watched.

We were there for an hour or so, talking and catching up, when a brawl erupted. Two gargantuan men were screaming at each other, their faces so close I believe they were actually trying to smell each other. The smelling led to pushing, with one man falling into a crowded table and sending drinks, glass, and patrons sprawling.

Shawn, being a regular, wasn't going to tolerate this in his bar. He jumped up and grabbed the closest participant – the man who had fallen into the table. He yanked him by the back of his jacket and his belt and hauled him out the door.

I, being a good friend and curious, followed them out.

Shawn roughly pushed the man forward and said to me, "You keep him out here. I'll go see what's going on with the other guy," and he ducked back inside.

Thus, I ended up in the street at midnight in a shady part of town with a slightly disoriented and very angry man.

He was shaking with rage and adrenaline. He paced rapidly, towards me and away, and on each lap towards me I was certain he was going to attack. He was muttering steadily, but he would punctuate it with occasional, loud utterances of the F-word. He was several inches taller than me and had decidedly more tattoos on his neck. He spat often, and I realized that he was spitting blood when some of his sputum refused to detach and fell down his chin and onto his shirt.

I was remarkably uncomfortable. In an attempt to deescalate the situation, I wanted to talk to the man. If we could find some common ground, maybe I could talk him down – or at least dissuade him from stomping me if necessary.

"Cold night," I tried.

He stopped pacing for a second and glared at me. "What the fuck did you just say to me?" he asked.

I tried to smile harmlessly and shrug, and he began pacing and mumbling again.

"What the fuck did I do to that guy?" he slurred. I wasn't sure whether or not he was talking to me, but I couldn't come up with a suitable response in any case.

"Hey," he said to me, "Do you have a cigarette?"

Damn Surgeon General! "No, sorry, I don't smoke."

He gave me a look of disgust.

It seemed that we could find no common ground. I was on the verge of giving up when he said, "Do you know the only reason why I don't go back in there and kill him? The only thing saving his life?" He paused and I shook my head. "I don't wanna go back to the pen."

At that moment, I felt all of the differences slip away and we were linked by this shared trait. We may not have much in common, but we certainly had this.

I leaned in to him, as if he were a conspirator.

"I know what you mean," I said softly. "I don't want to back to Penn either."

*

While I was finishing up my time at Columbia, the *Daily Pennsylvanian* – the student newspaper at Penn – published an article about my project. I was immediately grateful to the writers and editors, as well as to Todd for his help bringing attention to my return visit.

My next emotion as I read the piece was intrigue. I had been keeping and publishing a travelogue of my adventures online. The reporter was able to draw on my written observations about my time at Penn. Thus, the article revolved around the fact that I did not have a great experience during my first visit. It called my trip a "nightmare" – melodramatic maybe, but not inaccurate.

I loved that the article was different from the other articles on my project. It lacked the vanilla fluff of some of the other published stories and replaced it with silly jabs, including some from students that they interviewed at the other schools I had visited. A fine bit of writing with a twist that made it more interesting to me.

And then I saw the comments posted by the general public at the bottom of the online article. The public, it seemed, was very unhappy with me. There were a few themes that ran through the vitriolic comments.

One major theme was wondering whether or not I had actually attended Penn. Some people speculated that I had received my degree from Penn through correspondence courses – an option that I am confident was not available at this Ivy League institution. They were confused about why a person who attended Penn would need to return to the campus to explore it at all. Some of the commenters conducted research to determine whether or not I was really an alumnus as I claimed.

A few people wondered what grudge I was carrying or what axe I was grinding. Surely, I was out to get Penn from the get-go. How could I compare an urban campus like Penn to a rural one like Dartmouth? Where was my journalistic integrity?

A point that angered people to a level that stymied me was the fact that I mentioned that I had received "a ridiculous" number of parking tickets during my time at Penn. A select group of readers was incensed that I would judge a school based on my bad parking. How dare I say that I didn't have a good experience at Penn just because I received parking tickets!

The public was mostly anonymous and really cranky.

Not everyone was anonymous, however. For example, a member of the Penn Class of 1943 sent me an e-mail in which he dared me to come say bad things about

Penn to his face – a thinly veiled ruse, I'm sure, to get someone to visit him in his nursing home.

A couple of current students sent me e-mails in a challenging tone inviting me to let them show me around. I responded to most and accepted the challenge.

And then there was Barry – tour guide extraordinaire. The silly bastard made an attempt at anonymity by not including his name, but he provided enough detail that it was easy to pick him out.

Barry wrote some choice insults. I'd like to pretend that they didn't bother me, but they *really* did. You might think that I would feel better when I realized that the person writing the insults was a person about whom I already had a low opinion. But no. The fact that he insulted other students in the same post – and the fact that he was so outwardly obnoxious as to declare, "My Dad makes a lot of money" – did not soothe me, either. I'll admit: I lost some sleep.

The main reason I lost sleep is for my own stupidity. I could have lived a happy life without reading comments posted by what I imagined to be mentally deranged halfwits typing away angrily on their keyboards while sipping Yoo-hoo from spill-proof cups. I felt like I had seen something suspicious sitting in a clump on the sidewalk, and I stepped in it anyway. I should have known better.

I also lost sleep because the reactions to the article disappointed me. The insults and threats did not especially concern me as they landed – as a Marine, I am not so easily damaged – but they upset me as they were cast. Mine was a project of love. I was rooting for the people and the schools. The shortsightedness, meanness, and craziness of the posts left me discouraged and disheartened.

But I had made a commitment, and I had students waiting to show me what I had missed. The fallout of the article would just be another anecdote in my travels. I pledged to avoid reading future online comments, and I set off for Penn again.

*

I did not, however, go alone. Shawn drags me to Big Mike's; I haul him to Philadelphia.

We arrived on St. Patrick's Day. We rolled into town hungry, so it was good that our first appointment was with a small group of Penn undergrads at Abner's Cheesesteaks. We walked in and saw Todd at a table waving to us. We ordered our steaks – mine with, Shawn's without (onions, for those of you unfamiliar with the cheesesteak ordering convention) – and joined four students at a table. Todd introduced me to the group, and I introduced Shawn. The plan was to eat, head to a local bar for a drink with other classmates, and then attend a St. Patrick's Day party at an off-campus apartment in Hamilton Court.

After all of the anxiety leading up to my return, I was grateful for the opportunity to relax among Todd and his friends. I immediately felt the tide turning on my experience at Penn.

Less than two minutes into our sandwiches, one of the young women, Ann, said, "When I read the article about you, I really hated you, but I've calmed down since then."

"Yeah," Paula chimed in. "We are pretty tolerant. You just need to watch out for Mason at the party. He's really pissed about you being here."

"And a lot of the girls I know are angry, too," Ann added with a tone of helpfulness.

I suppose it was helpful in some ways. It gave Shawn a chuckle as only a true friend can have at the discomfort of his comrade. Moreover, it provided me some ideas of people to avoid – including the wide category of "girls." I was suddenly glad that my cheesesteak with onions weaponized my breath for the evening.

The warnings and my breath were all for naught. We went to the Blarney Stone and met up with a dozen or so Penn seniors. Every person I talked to wanted to talk about the article. No one seemed outwardly angry about it. Many had clarifying questions, and I had the impression that perhaps every student walked away feeling a bit better about my project. A few people were eager to dish the school, commiserating with my reported experiences or heaping on their own negative observations. I had great conversations with warm and welcoming students, most of whom loved Penn and were happy to share the best parts with me. The best parts of Penn, according to this crowd, had two themes.

The first "best part" was the social scene. As they defined it, I understood why I may have missed it in my first visit. I suppose I was looking for the socializing I saw at Dartmouth where the students are isolated in a small community through long winters; or at Yale where the residential system and safety of the campus tend to pull people together. At Penn, it was not so much about the university itself as it was having young, smart, and often affluent people living in a city as vibrant as Philadelphia. The university certainly provided events and activities. Those activities were fine, according to this group, but they were not at the core of the socialization. At a school as large as Penn – a giant in the Ivy League – undergrads can form friendships that are not forced by proximity, but developed through shared interests. Furthermore, the grip that Penn holds on its community is more tenuous. A 15-minute walk from campus at Cornell would land you in a gorge, a field, or a residential neighborhood – and in any of them, you would be identifiable as a Cornell student. A short walk from Penn's campus would take you into a major city with all of its allure, and you could lose yourself or reinvent yourself there.

The Things I Learned in College

Thus, it is the off-campus nightlife with like-minded friends that makes Penn so special – according to this group of like-minded friends hanging out off-campus.

The second "best part" was the opportunity at Penn. Like the social point, I could see in retrospect how this might have been hidden from me. I had grown accustomed to seeing the professional opportunities from my vantage point on campus, but many of the more interesting prospects came from Philadelphia. For example, I had met students at other schools who were active volunteers in non-profits; but, at Penn, students could work with the headquarters of major organizations. While an undergrad at another school might have a prestigious summer job, a Penn student could serve as an intern at a major corporation, law firm, or consulting company around the edges of their school work during the year. Every student that engaged me in a discussion of the opportunities at Penn was availing his or herself of those opportunities. A fashion student was working one-on-one with a hot designer across the city; a Wharton junior had a paid externship at Deloitte; an undergrad who was waiting to hear whether he was admitted to Penn's School of Veterinary Medicine had a part-time job at the Philadelphia Zoo; just to name a few. While I personally favor a more insular environment, the benefits of a major metropolitan area are compelling.

The conversations at the bar were helpful to my research. I learned more about the University of Pennsylvania, and I did it from the mouths of those who were fortunate and accomplished enough to attend the school.

The party in Hamilton Court on Chestnut Street proved to be equally useful, but in different ways. Shawn and I rode a small elevator to the seventh floor where we found a fantastic apartment full of young people. The balcony overlooked the City of Philadelphia and was

172

clogged with party guests wanting to see the view. The mood was relaxed, and people were drinking and talking.

I was happy to see that many of the people I had met and liked previously were there. Not only was Todd with us, but many of the students he had introduced me to at the end of my last trip were there as well. Gretchen was at the party, and she had brought two friends. The friends were both women studying at Princeton. They were tall and gorgeous, eager to hear about my project. They were glad to talk to Shawn and me for the majority of the night. Not only did I get to experience a genuinely social moment at Penn, but I also got to make connections at Princeton.

The only iffy moment occurred when Mason – angry Mason who was infuriated by my previous experiences at Penn – arrived at the party. Ann interrupted our conversation with the Princeton women to announce, with a gleam in her eye, that Mason was in the hall and wanted to speak with me. I could hear loud, drunken singing in the hallway by the elevators – someone was singing the Penn fight song – and Ann nodded towards the singing.

I excused myself from the conversation and headed towards the hall. The door burst open as I approached it. A big kid popped through the door and stopped at the sight of me, the song frozen on his lips. "Are you the writer?" he asked.

"Yep."

It turned out he had consumed enough alcohol to get angry and express that anger in song, but that was the extent of it. "Oh. Cool," he replied sheepishly. He turned and walked back out the door quietly, and I never encountered him again.

*

The next morning, Shawn left for home and I went to meet a group of biology students in Leidy Labs behind the Quad. The students were meeting on this Saturday morning with a teaching assistant who was in the second year of her Ph.D. program. It was not a regularly scheduled meeting, but these undergrads wanted some extra preparation in advance of an exam the following week. These were biology majors who had advanced beyond the introductory courses that were used to weed out the future doctors from the wannabes.

I joined the group late and listened to the question and answer session. When it wrapped up, a young man with perfect blonde hair and wearing an athletic jacket approached me, introducing himself for the first time in person. His name was Bobby, and he had contacted me after the release of the article. He was hand-in-hand with a young woman – blonder and also wearing an athletic jacket – improbably named Bobbi. Bobby and Bobbi were a Penn power couple: Both juniors, both biology majors, and both athletes – track for him and diving for her. They were an impressive couple, heartwarming if you did not dwell on the fact that their many similarities made them appear more like siblings than lovers.

We walked and talked through the science buildings. They showed me the labs in Leidy and Goddard – including two separate labs where each had experiments brewing. Bobby was working as a part of a team with three other biology students on an experiment involving the development of viruses. This work was part of a class, but the teams were all tackling different projects. This term-length experiment would be part of a showcase in April alongside the work of their classmates. The success of this project would open doors to participate on grant-funded experiments next year. Bobbi, on the other hand, was conducting research in partnership with a senior faculty member. The subject was the way that white blood cells respond to multiple targets, and the goal was publication in a major academic or medical journal. Bobbi's take, however, was that the value was simply working one-on-one with a distinguished faculty member.

We walked through John Morgan, the Johnson Building, and Stemmler Hall before passing into the Hospital of the University of Pennsylvania Health System. These buildings are part of the School of Medicine. Bobby and Bobbi intended to apply the next year, but both hoped to be admitted to Duke's School of Medicine. Penn Medicine is the oldest medical school in the country – and certainly one of the best – but the Bobbies were from the south, and they hoped to return closer to home for the next stage of their academic journey.

As we talked about medical school, we circled back along Hamilton Walk behind the Quad and in front of the science buildings. We slipped between the buildings and ended up in one of my favorite Penn spots: Kaskey Park. If you did not know where to look for it, you might never find it – a quiet and clean bit of woods with a small pond, footpaths, and plenty of benches.

I left them in this romantic space, and headed to my next destination. I had a series of meetings with students to look at housing: From the Quad to the fraternities to the high-rises to houses along Spruce and Pine Streets. I had a fleet of undergrads willing to open their homes to me. I could have stayed longer with any one of them, but I was trying to cram as much as possible into a short period of time.

I went straight from my housing tour to a production of the Mask and Wig Club. Mask and Wig is an all-male comedy group that puts on annual shows that draw Penn students, Penn alumni, and plenty of parents to their clubhouse across town. The production was original and well done. I laughed my fair share and admired the talent of the performers. At the end, I blushed when they announced from the stage that I was in the audience – part of a ritual of announcing all known attendees.

175

For me, a sign of a well done show is that it leaves me with a clear memory of some line or bit. In this case, I walked away with a popular jingle stuck in my head that would remind me of the show every time I heard it in the years that followed. To the cast and crew associated with the show: Bravo!

Sunday morning, I met with six faculty members for brunch. They talked and laughed, they demonstrated keen wits and sharp minds, and they answered questions and told stories. Many were curious about what I had found at other schools, and they wanted to discuss the differences between the other Ivies and Penn – both what I had found and their observations. They invited me to additional classes, athletic events, and social activities.

They were all so engaging and charming that I would have accepted every offer if I had the time.

*

So, you might wonder, where does this leave us?

I am glad that I went back. The fact that people took the time to try to correct the record is not lost on me. I saw activities – and, more importantly, I met people – that I missed the first time through. That made it worthwhile.

Part of my satisfaction comes from simply doing the hard thing. I sometimes describe my time in the Marine Corps as a better thing to have done than to do. I love having challenges behind me where I can begin to look back on them with nostalgia and begin to miss the good parts and minimize the bad. With the Penn chapter behind me, I had earned a story that had lost its power to ruin my day.

I was a fan of Penn going into this endeavor – a big enough fan that I personally chose this school over others that I might have attended. I am still a fan. A trip to Philadelphia is never complete for me until I walk around the campus, stopping in the student store to buy some sort of a Penn knick-knack, and making a quick turn around the pond in Kaskey Park. The university is world-class, and I am proud of my affiliation with it.

Driving away from Penn, I reflected again on the article in the *Daily Pennsylvanian*. I especially thought about the interview that I gave to the reporter who wrote the story. She – like many Penn students – was surprised that my first visit left a bad taste in my mouth. I could not deny that it was disappointing, but I felt bad when she confirmed incredulously, "So, we were the school you enjoyed the least?"

I responded lightly and with words that she used to conclude her article. "Hey," I said, "there's still Harvard."

The Things I Learned in College

HARVARD UNIVERSITY

Q: How many Harvard students does it take to screw in a light bulb?

A: One – he just holds it up and the world turns around him.

Thus, I arrived at a pivotal point in my project. When I speak to people about my journey, the chapter that piques the most interest is Harvard. People are hungry for information and tales from this institution.

Some of the curiosity came from the student scholars I met at the other Ivies. Many students self-selected not to apply to Harvard; many others were not offered a space in the class. When students spoke about Harvard, I sometimes noted a wistfulness or bitterness that did not often arise in conversations about the other schools.

The majority of the curiosity, however, can be attributed to the fact that people have heard of the university. Harvard is the granddaddy of brands in the Ivy League and higher education in general. Its name is recognized around the world. Many people can even find it on a map – a feat not easily duplicated at other schools. Many people would have a tough time finding Columbia University on the globe, even spotting them "in the City of New York."

The name "Harvard" represents the embodiment of the Ivies. Whatever the Ivy League has, Harvard must have the most of it; whatever the Ivy League is, Harvard must be *it* the most. The smartest, the richest, the snobbiest, the hottest, the nerdiest – Harvard must be the epitome of every quality.

This was the chapter that I knew people would flip to upon finding my book. I was determined to do it right.

*

Harvard is a complicated business entity. It employs more than 4,000 faculty and 8,000 staff to serve over 20,000 undergraduate and graduate students, making it the largest employer in Cambridge, Massachusetts and one of the largest in the Boston area. Setting aside the enterprise of education involving faculty teaching learners in classrooms – which is much more complicated than it may appear at a glance – a research university also includes a hospital, a police force, food service operations, and dozens of buildings. The Widener Library and the university library system at Harvard is the largest at any university in the world. Harvard generates and spends hundreds of millions of dollars each year, and it sports the largest endowment of any university in the world – measured in the tens of billions of dollars.

Someone has to run this business. Each unit must be managed and functions must receive oversight, but it must all boil up to a single person's leadership and vision.

During my time at Harvard, the president was Lawrence "Larry" Summers. Summers was an economic rock star on a level appropriate to running one of the world's leading universities.

Let's start by considering his family: His parents were both economics professors at Penn. Impressive for a person who would become an economist, but there's more: Two of his uncles – one on *each side* of his family – won Nobel Prizes in economics.

Summers completed his undergraduate work at MIT and earned a Ph.D. at Harvard where he began teaching. He won many prestigious awards and earned tenure when he was only 28 years old – nearly a record at Harvard.

Despite having tenure – which guarantees job security in higher education – he left academia to become the Chief Economist at the World Bank. He served in this role for two years before joining President Bill Clinton's administration in the Treasury Department. Ultimately, Summers became the 71st Secretary of the Treasury.

So here we have a person who had the family pedigree and the academic credentials of a world class scholar. He had led complicated bureaucracies in the national spotlight. When you add on the other traits that Summers shared with other Harvard presidents – he was a white male, which all Harvard presidents had been, and he personally earned a Harvard degree, which was a tradition since 1672 – he seemed the very picture of a Harvard president.

Universities, however, can be hotbeds of politics. I don't mean republicans versus democrats; I mean ridiculously smart people who are in the business of provocation and pushing boundaries, and who are interacting in close proximity to each other. People have the time and intellect to engage in epic struggles around issues big and small. There are factions and agendas and negotiations and deals and power struggles. No president has it easy.

One might argue that Summers had it worse than some. Despite the incredible achievements and genetics that brought him to the presidency, he had one glaring weakness: Communication. It seemed that when Larry opened his mouth, either his foot went in or an apology came out.

The biggest and most relevant example was the incident involving women in science and engineering. In January, Summers accepted an invitation to speak at a conference sponsored by the National Bureau of Economic Research. The conference was dedicated to furthering the diversification of people working in science and engineering – fields dominated by men. Summers's talk was on the topic of why women may be underrepresented in tenured positions in these fields at top universities.

There are two views of what happened when he spoke.

The first was that he asserted that women may simply lack the aptitude for science and engineering that men have. In other words, women just aren't as gifted as men. Those who heard this heard that women were the inferior sex.

The second view was that he was a tenured professor enjoying the academic freedom that comes with this position. He prefaced his remarks on aptitude by explicitly stating that he was trying to provoke reactions – presumably an outrage that could be channeled into creating change. He went on to discuss how to bring more women into the fields of science and engineering. His bit about aptitude was just one piece of an overall talk designed to help correct the dearth of women in these fields.

The talk drew harsh criticism. Summers apologized in the weeks that followed.

In March, less than a week before I landed on campus, the other shoe dropped. Harvard is composed of many academic units, the biggest of which is the Faculty of Arts and Sciences. The Faculty had a meeting and a vote of "no confidence" in the leadership of the president was called. The motion passed 218–185.

The Board of the Harvard Corporation – the only people who can hire or fire the president – issued statements of support for Summers. Faculty and students on both sides of the debate spoke out. Larry continued to apologize but said that he would not heed the calls for him to resign his post.

It was into this turmoil and contention that I thrust myself.

(Larry Summers was president when I arrived, and he was president when I left, but he did not make it too much longer. Less than a year later, he announced his resignation from the presidency at Harvard. He went on to great things – not the least of which was to accept an appointment as a University Professor at Harvard, which is both rare and prestigious – and he went on to additional controversy. After an interim period, Harvard named Summers's successor: Drew Gilpin Faust. Faust is another incredible academic rock star, but she breaks the mold in two respects: One, she is the first woman to hold the presidency at Harvard; and two, she is the first Harvard President in over 300 years to *not* hold a degree from Harvard.)

*

Although I made good use of Columbia's spring break by returning to Penn, I landed at Harvard just before students dispersed on break. There was no helping it: Spring breaks happen, and the Ivies go on break during different weeks. I was still so tired from an academic year of exploration that I was secretly glad for a week off.

During the course of this week, the *Crimson* – Harvard's newspaper – released an article about my project. The article included quotes from the anonymous feedback section of the Penn article – following me like a bad smell – but it did not include any contact information for me. Nevertheless, I had faith in the ability of Harvard undergrads to Google my name and reach out. The article was a necessary win because at this point I still had not talked to a single Harvard student. But there it was in black and white and crimson: I was on campus.

It is funny how the articles in the various student-run newspapers are received. At some schools, an article yielded hundreds of contacts; others only prompted a dozen or so messages that I would leverage to meet more and more people.

The article in the *Crimson* generated no messages from Harvard students. Not one.

I went back through some of the contacts I had made along the way: Heather at Cornell, Todd at Penn, Linda at Yale, etc. Many of them had made introductions for me at other schools. They seemed to have a network of contacts from high school or transfer students. I already had a short list of contacts in my pocket for my upcoming visit to Princeton.

No one had any contacts at Harvard, though. It helped to explain why Harvard was such a source of curiosity for the undergrads I talked to at other schools.

Upon returning from break and still having had no contact with students, I went to plan C. I created simple flyers. The body had a brief description of my project, and each flyer had five tear-off tabs with my contact information at the bottom. Harvard offered plenty of places to publicly display this sort of information, so I papered the campus and prepared for the onslaught of e-mails

When I received no messages after a few days, I went to check on the state of my flyers. I imagined that perhaps they had all been removed. To my surprise, they all seemed to be exactly where I left them. More to my surprise, they were all in exactly the same condition in which I left them. Not one tab was taken off of any flyer; not one moustache was penned on the picture of me.

I was not out of ideas.

I had contacted the administration at Harvard, just as I had at every institution. I could reach out and see what sort of help they could offer. It felt inequitable, however, to go this route. I had not relied on "official" help from an institution – including at Penn, where it was offered and where it could have been useful.

I also could have advertised beyond my flyers. I could have taken out ads in the *Crimson* or produced radio ads or hired a skywriter. But, again, I did not want to treat Harvard differently from other schools. I was there, and my presence was announced. It should be enough.

I had a final tactic up my sleeve: Accosting. I walked and sat and ate next to Harvard students every day. All I had to do was to approach someone and say, "Hello. Do you have a minute to hear what I am doing?" This strategy was always an option, but I was disinclined to use it. It was just a shade beyond my comfort zone, crossing from researcher to pest. It also exposed me to too much danger of rejection. Some people are built to hear "no" over and over until they get a "yes," but not me – especially with fresh wounds from the University of Pennsylvania.

To some extent, the silence was refreshing. I no longer had to be "on" all of the time. I did not risk discovering that my roommate was a drug addict or that my breakfast partner was an anti-Semite or that my next meeting would be with the marching band. I was tired from my time as a transient undergrad, and I could see the end drawing near. If I were living the full lifecycle of an undergraduate compressed into a single academic year, I suppose my attitude could be described as senioritis.

Friends and acquaintances were sometimes irate with my refusal to become more aggressive in pursuit of my mission. They gave me advice, and when that didn't work, they gave me lectures. They pushed me to try something – anything – to break into social circles. What would I write about in the Harvard chapter, they asked, if I did not meet any students?

Well, we will find out because for 30 days, more than a dozen classes, and hundreds of hours, I did not meet with a single Harvard student.

*

My lack of a social life left me with plenty of time for academics. On every campus, I attended classes. I even studied and completed assignments at times. At Harvard, though, I had even more time to indulge in my love of learning.

A retired Harvard professor who owned a house close to the school allowed me to use his driveway to park, saving me somewhere in the neighborhood of $48,000 in parking costs for the month. I would leave my car at his house and walk over to Harvard Square. Sometimes I would swing by the Au Bon Pain shop in the Square and sit among the Harvard community, watching people reading and preparing for class. When I was ready, I would dash across Massachusetts Avenue and through the gate between Wadsworth and Wigglesworth Halls – the second oldest building and the second biggest freshmen dorm, respectively.

Once inside, I was looking at the Old Yard. I stopped inside the gate and smiled. One of my most pleasant experiences at Harvard, and at every urban campus, was the moment I entered the campus. The safety was palpable.

Even with my eyes closed, I could tell it was springtime. The smells of flowers and fertilizer were heavy in the air. The trees were sprouting new leaves, and many were aflame with bright blossoms. Grounds workers were diligent in cleaning up the campus from a long winter. Flower beds were being maintained and enhanced.

Before me was a tree-lined green space, crisscrossed with paved walking paths, culminating at the top of the green at the red brick, four-story structure of Holworthy Hall. The building was one of the freshmen dorms, and it was in good company. To my left, I could see bits of other freshmen dorms through the trees.

Walking towards Holworthy, the Johnston Gate – looking very similar to the red brick and black wrought iron of the Van Wickle Gates at Brown University – came into view on my left.

Also on my left was another dorm: Massachusetts Hall. Built in 1720, this brick building is the oldest building at Harvard and the second oldest academic building in the United States. To put the age and significance of the building into perspective, residents of the dormitory have included John Adams, James Otis, and John Hancock. The building is not only a freshmen dorm, but also the office of the university president and upper administration.

For all of that, I rarely spent much time looking to the left. A building to my right grabbed and held my attention. The massive white granite of University Hall pulled me in. Actually, it was not the building itself – although the white color sat in appealing contrast to all of the red brick at the university – but it was the statue in front of it that always made me look.

The statue portrays John Harvard sitting in a chair with a book on his lap and two more within reach under his chair. The statue is bronze, weathered into blackness, save the tip of the statue's left foot that gleams like new. The six foot tall granite plinth under the statue has several seals and markings. On one side is the Harvard seal with the Latin word *Veritas* meaning "truth of character" shown on three open books; on another side is the seal of Emmanuel College at Cambridge University, the alma mater of John Harvard.

It is the inscription on the front of the plinth, however, that makes the statue notorious. The inscription simply reads: John Harvard · Founder · 1638. And because of this inscription, the statue is often called "the statue of three lies."

The first lie is that John was not the founder of Harvard. The school had already been founded upon the vote of the Great and General Court of Massachusetts Bay Colony. John Harvard made a sizeable donation to the institution, including over three hundred books, but he did not found the university.

The second lie of the legend is that Harvard was not founded in 1638. The vote that created the university was taken in 1636. Harvard is the first university in the territory that would become the United States 140 years later, but the date on the statue is off by two years.

The final lie is that the statue does not actually depict John Harvard. In 1884 when the statue was created

187

– just as today – no one had any idea what John Harvard really looked like. So the creator had a Harvard student, Sherman Hoar, pose as a model. Thus, in the absence of a better model, they chose some random Hoar.

The biggest lie, however, is evident in the shine on John's left shoe. Visitors were told that they should rub the left foot of the statue for luck. While I am not offended by such a tradition, I am surprised that it developed so recently. People have only been rubbing that particular appendage since the 1990s. In addition, it is only outsiders who are copping a feel. Harvard students know better. Their interactions with the statue are confined to Commencement when they remove their caps as they pass the statue on their way to graduation.

If Harvard students don't touch the statue, how do you suppose the toe has gone from black to shiny?

The answer also explains why my eye was drawn to the statue. Harvard, unlike any school that I had experienced, draws tourists. Many, many tourists. On a typical day in any daylight hour, there was a line of people waiting to touch the foot and pose for pictures. Sometimes these were families and prospective students, but often they were sight-seers with not even a hopeful future affiliation with the university. They just wanted to see and touch and experience Harvard.

It is funny that I viewed these crowds with a bit of scorn. They were practically my kin, dedicating an afternoon where I was devoting months. I should have embraced them and stepped up as the ruler of this class of bizarre voyeurs, but instead I would shake my head and hurry by.

Behind University Hall, I could see the outside of Widener Library. The library was named in memory of Harvard alumnus and collector of books, Harry Elkins Widener, who died in the sinking of the *RMS Titanic* in 1912. If I had to pick a second regret beyond not interacting with undergraduates at Harvard, it would be that I never had an opportunity to explore Widener. I am confident that I could have spent hours and hours exploring the contents and rooms of the library. One artifact of special note is a complete Gutenberg Bible, one of only about 20 complete bibles printed in or around 1450.

My usual routine was to turn away from Widener Library and trek across the green to the Memorial Church. With its four-pillared front porch under a white steeple, it was a building that I could almost always enter and find quiet. The building was a tribute to Harvard community members who died while in service of their country in time of war. The names of those who had died were carved high into the interior granite block walls. The list of names for World War II was expansive, reaching back to the class of 1904 with Franklin Delano Roosevelt's name among the dead. FDR was one of seven U.S. presidents at the time of my visit who were Harvard men. I may not have been either a president or a Harvard man, but I felt a sense of belonging at a memorial to service members.

I would sit in silence – or perhaps allowing the music of a practicing organist to wash over me – and plan my activities for the day.

I sat in on about 15 courses during my short stay at Harvard. I chose them based on my own interests, comments I found online, or occasionally intercepted bits of information that I eavesdropped. Sometimes the classes were great; sometimes not.

On one occasion, I stepped out of the church in the afternoon and encountered a short line winding into Sever Hall next door. I went over to join the line to see what was happening. I asked the gentleman in front of me where the line was heading. He replied that a psychology class was having a guest speaker – a famous neurosurgeon and writer – and that the lecture was being held in a larger room and open to the public.

"Have you ever heard him speak?" asked the man.

"No," I admitted.

His eyes rolled up into his head in rapture. "He is amazing! One of the best speakers I ever heard."

The opinion of this stranger sold me. I stood in muted excitement for 10 minutes before winning a seat in the middle of the lecture hall.

The renowned scientist took the stage. He also took an hour of my life that I cannot get back. His talk had definite high points – including showing us the amazing illustrations of buildings created by an autistic savant, and discussing his relationship with a famous comedian – but it was generally painful. He commented several times that he did not know how to organize the talk, but I had already figured that out. Two minutes before the scheduled end of the talk, he blurted, "Oops! This talk is supposed to be about the brain, and I just realized that I haven't said anything about the brain yet."

At the end of the talk, the scientist prepared to take questions, but I exploded out of my seat and ran for it. I had survived, but just barely.

Most of my academic experiences at Harvard, however, were much better.

I sat in on a course in mathematics that was taught by a young and entertaining professor. The course had hundreds of students, and math is not my strong suit, but the professor brought the material to life. In mere weeks, I was tackling abstract concepts and completing mathematical proofs that should have been beyond me. He almost had me convinced that I had missed my calling as a mathematician.

I had a similar experience in music. I do not play an instrument – at all – but I tended to haunt the music courses during my stay. I was amazed at the aptitude of the pupils and the accomplishments of the professors. As you might imagine, Harvard does not abide by slackers. In a field such as music, with output that is so tangible and experiential, I was able to appreciate the awesome talent of the people involved. I'll admit that after weeks of listening to lectures and practices and demonstrations, I sidled up to a piano and tapped away on the keys. I figured I might have acquired some flair for music by osmosis, or perhaps I was a musical genius with some latent talent that had never been tapped.

I didn't and I wasn't.

In a computer science class, we discussed Facebook. The site had only been live for a year or so when I visited. It started at Harvard and was only open to Harvard students before expanding to all Ivy League schools and a few select other institutions at the time of this class. It was a subject of talk at other schools I had visited – at Cornell, several students showed me their profiles on Facebook; at Brown, a couple of undergrads talked with me about the differences between Facebook and the Brown social media, the Daily Jolt; by Yale, everyone seemed to be on it – but this talk was different in three ways.

First, in a computer science class, the group was discussing the code. It was an open conversation where students were making pitches about how to modify the code to achieve additional functionality. The professor was challenging them to think both in terms of function and marketability. It was like an early laboratory for what would become computer applications.

Second, the talk of using the site to "poke" people gave rise to many funny moments. As one young man exclaimed, blushing behind his glasses, "I was poked once, and she was really hot!"

The final difference between this conversation and others was that some of these classmates knew the players involved in creating Facebook. A couple claimed to know or remember Mark Zuckerberg, and one angry student piped up occasionally saying, "Mark stole this whole thing anyway!" The student was a member of the crew team and knew the Winklevoss twins – Cameron and

Tyler – who claimed to have been the original conceivers of the site. At the time, Facebook was just another Web site, but in retrospect, it was an interesting conversation to overhear.

I sat in on a course led by a teaching fellow in Art History and nearly fell in love. The course was on landscape architecture in the ancient world. The material was entrancing. The class examined images – focused on minute details or wide, sweeping shots – of ancient gardens. We discussed the practical and aesthetic considerations that went into the gardens, and we relied on science, theory, and plenty of imagination. As I sat in the class, I became enchanted by the image of me walking through ancient ruins, making new discoveries with a magnifying glass and a fine brush – and perhaps a whip, because this fantasy always devolved into something having to do with Indiana Jones.

But, to be frank, I was equally smitten with the instructor. Her smile was infectious, her voice was soothing, and her intellect was appealing. I sat in rapt attention, listening to her discuss in esoteric detail the wonders of far-away lands, and occasionally slipping into a daydream where the two of us were trapped in a crypt filled with snakes.

I only went to the class once. My isolation at Harvard left me too susceptible to the allure of this graduate student.

Some of my favorite classes at Harvard were in the sciences. I found several remarkable courses in the gargantuan Harvard University Science Center just to the north of Harvard Yard. I spent time in labs and lectures in physics and chemistry, enjoying the experience of becoming more knowledgeable in these subjects.

I also wanted to sit through a course on biology. I identified the course I wanted, slipped into the large lecture hall, and took a seat beside a young Harvard student. I pulled out my notebook and prepared to learn.

The girl beside me turned and locked eyes with me. *Oh boy,* I thought, *a Harvard student is getting ready to strike up a conversation with me!*

She leaned in and said, "You can't."

"What?" I asked.

With more urgency: "You *can't.*"

"I'm sorry, I don't understand."

"You can't sit there."

I was thoroughly confused until I noticed that no two students were sitting side-by-side. The professor and teaching assistants were moving through the aisles passing out paper booklets.

"Is there a test today?" The girl beside me and several other students in the vicinity nodded yes. I snapped my notebook shut and stood abruptly, saying a bit louder than I intended, "I'm out of here!"

The laughter and applause of the students made my day.

*

I may not have met with any Harvard students, but that does not mean that I did not meet with *any* students.

My love for higher education is not confined to the Ivy League. I am passionate about learning among the brightest and most ambitious in their fields. This type of environment exists at the Ivies, but it is also present at other highly selective institutions.

When I was at Brown University, I was fascinated by the people at RISD. The Rhode Island School of Design is as impressive as Brown in terms of selectivity, famous alumni, and resources. The students are as brilliant as they are artistic, which made them exceptionally fun to encounter. The piece that I find captivating to the point of taking my breath away is that Brown and RISD are so close together. Such talent and potential sharing the same hill in Providence, Rhode Island!

I lacked contacts at Harvard, but my friend Linda at Yale offered to introduce me to a couple of students at MIT: The Massachusetts Institute of Technology.

MIT is fascinating in many ways. First, it was a beneficiary of the Morrill Land-Grant Colleges Act of 1862. Under this act, one school in each state received 30,000 acres of land that it could use or sell "to promote the liberal and practical education of the industrial classes in the several pursuits and professions in life." Almost every school benefitting under the Morrill Land-Grant is a public institution, but MIT, as a highly selective private institution, is a notable exception. (You may recall that Cornell University is a second exception to this rule, and it is the only Ivy to also serve as a Land-Grant school.) The Massachusetts Institute of Technology is also noteworthy for its independence. Harvard made several attempts in the late nineteenth and early twentieth centuries to force MIT into a merger. MIT was financially weak, but it stood its ground and remained separated from its older, bigger, and richer brother.

The two main related reasons why I am intrigued by MIT is its selectivity and weirdness.

The academic rigor of the place is beyond reproach. One cannot spit without hitting a Nobel laureate. (You should not test this principle – the laureates tend to get grumpy when spat upon.) The students are gifted and accomplished. In the sciences and engineering, MIT is unsurpassed.

The oddity of the school can be seen all over, including in its architecture. The year before my visit, MIT opened its Strata Center. I could try to describe it, but I could not do better than Robert Campbell did when he penned this *positive* review in the *Boston Globe*: "[The Strata] looks as if it's about to collapse. Columns tilt at scary angles. Walls teeter, swerve, and collide in random curves and angles. Materials change wherever you look: brick, mirror-surface steel, brushed aluminum, brightly

194

colored paint, corrugated metal. Everything looks improvised, as if thrown up at the last moment."

Another sign of the culture at MIT is that, while most MIT students would be able to direct you to the Strata, that is not necessarily what they would call it. They would call it Building 32. MIT buildings have names and numbers, but the numbers are pervasive.

The delicious strangeness goes beyond the buildings. The class rings worn by alumni vary from year to year, but they are all inscribed with the initials IHTFP. These letters also factor into various student pieces across campus. The letters represent the unofficial but well-known school motto: "I hate this fucking place." People who are offended by the profanity may claim that the letters mean, "It's hard to fondle penguins" – as if that were any better – or "I help tutor freshmen physics."

On a warm April day, I went to meet with a group of MIT undergrads.

I had been jogging around Cambridge in an effort to find my way around town. The Boston area is notoriously complicated in its road system, which is based on old cow paths, according to the myth. MIT is only a mile or so from Harvard. I scheduled my meeting with the students at the tail end of a run.

I started in Harvard Square and set out to see as much of Harvard as I could. I ran through Harvard Yard, around the buildings of the Law School and the School of Engineering and Applied Sciences, and over to the Divinity School. I looped over to the Quad that used to house Radcliffe College – the women's college that was not formally merged into Harvard until 1999 – and down to the Graduate School of Education. I looped back, crossing the Charles River on the John W. Weeks pedestrian bridge, and jogged around the stadium and the Harvard Business School. I considered trying to find my way to the medical and dental schools, but they were more than three miles away, and I had an appointment to keep.

I ran back to the Charles and followed the river past the beautiful and mysterious housing for Harvard upperclassmen. One of my favorite parts of Harvard – and I would argue the favorite part of any sane observer – was the colorful cupolas atop Lowell and Dunster Houses. The blue of the former and crimson of the latter were bright and beautiful. I understand that the housing system at Harvard was not unlike that at Yale, with 12 houses that students occupy after their freshmen year. I would have loved to have explored those buildings with the people who lived there.

Instead, I ran while glancing at the Harvard buildings to my left. I continued jogging until I saw the Great Dome of MIT's Building 10 on the horizon. I slowed to a walk and ambled towards my meeting on the grass in front of the famous building.

Linda's friends, George and Pierre, were waiting for me. They had brought an army of friends to meet me – at least 20 students. They had blankets and coolers and books and laptop computers spread out on the grass.

It took me a minute to realize what was missing. They had no Frisbees, baseball equipment, or Nerf footballs. Despite the nice weather, this group was not out to engage in heavy physical activity. They were pasty in complexion – even the African American students – and doughy in physique. I counted 14 computers, three pocket protectors, and a Rubik's Cube.

As I was introduced to Skippy, Scooter, Chester, Dexter, and the gang, I realized that I had arranged a date with a gaggle of nerds. These certainly were not the first bookish students I had encountered in my travels, but it made me more self-conscious of my athletic gear doused in sweat.

Like many of the people I met on my journey, they started out with an air of cynicism, but they quickly warmed to me and my project. They offered and I accepted a bottle of water and a peanut butter and jelly sandwich.

We sat in the sun and talked about MIT and my adventures. After the lack of connections I experienced at Harvard, I was grateful for their generosity and interest.

Eventually, I brought the talk around to a key area of inquiry for me. "So, do any of you know any Harvard students I could talk to?"

They all looked at each other. "Well, my ex-boyfriend goes to Harvard," volunteered a girl wearing about three pounds too much makeup, "but he's my *ex*-boyfriend. You wouldn't want to talk to him."

"I know some people," said Chester, "but only to see them. I don't know their contact info or anything."

Another undergrad spoke up. "Yeah, I'm in a class at Harvard, and I have some Harvard students in my classes here, but I don't socialize with them."

And so it went. The MIT students stated that they did not interact much with the Harvard students.

On the back of that discussion, however, my new friends began talking about Harvard students. I had heard people across the Ivy League speculate and generalize about people at the other schools, including Harvard. What I found especially compelling about this particular conversation was the proximity and exposure of this group to Harvard students.

"Harvard students are so serious!" mused a young woman called Skippy. She wore a loose-fitting hippie dress, hippopotamus slippers, and glasses with thick frames and thicker lenses that gave her a cross-eyed appearance.

"Yeah," a classmate agreed. "I'm surprised they don't crack more often."

I had always thought of MIT students as especially uptight. "They are under more stress than you?"

"Academically, it's probably the same," said Skippy. "We're pretty geeky when it comes to school . . ."

"*Nooo*," I protested.

197

". . . but they are stressed about life, and we are just stressed about school."

"You won't find them hanging out like this," said Pierre with a sweep of his hand at the assembled mass.

I was doubtful. I ran by many Harvard students that morning.

But then George clarified, "You might see them outside, but they will be throwing a ball of some sort at each other. They always need to be competing and pushing. They want to be the best at everything."

Around a bite of sandwich, Skippy good-naturedly confided to me, "They won't sit around eating peanut butter sandwiches with you."

Well, that was the truth!

"I like how driven they are, though," said another student. "I admire that."

The group went on to talk about how attractive, smart, and ambitious the scholars at Harvard were. They did not seem at all self-conscious or embarrassed by the conversation. They had generally positive things to say about their comrades up the river.

"Did any of you want to go to Harvard?" I asked.

None jumped at the bait. "We're not the Harvard type," Pierre said. "I think we are plenty smart enough, but we are too..." He drifted off in search of a word.

"Fun," offered Skippy, and the others agreed.

I lacked a basis for comparison, but they might have been on to something. They showed me around campus, and that night I accompanied them to a party in the exceedingly bizarre-looking Simmons Hall. I laughed harder with them than I had in weeks. Skippy turned out to be a poet of some talent – unexpected in a chemical engineering major – and Pierre not only studied theoretical physics, but could juggle almost any object that was thrown his way. They were nerds – with the spelling bee trophies to prove it – but they were blessedly kind and self-aware.

And, yes, they were fun.

*

I was surprised by the number of homeless people – many of whom appeared to be college-aged kids – who congregated in Harvard Square just outside the walls of the school. I did not know where they came from or why they chose that location to hang out. It was a different type of dispossessed person than I saw other places. Whatever sickness, bad luck, or choices that brought them to this place, the majority of them seemed to socialize with each other. By and large, they lacked the loneliness and solitude that I associated with homelessness.

They also seemed to be more engaged with the public walking by them. Sometimes they served as street performers. (Or maybe I confused street performers for them.) They begged for change, sold pens, and otherwise solicited. Occasionally, they harangued.

One evening, I walked through the Square deep in thought. I was coming from a lecture given by a professor at the John F. Kennedy School of Government – a professor who had recently won the Pulitzer Prize for her writings on genocide. The subject was heavy, and my head was swimming.

"Hey, you!" said a voice coming from too close. I turned to see two men walking in stride with me. One was decidedly older than the other, but both were dressed in grimy clothes and heavy coats. Both had rough beards. "Give me a dollar!" mumbled the older man.

In response to his gruff directive, I merely replied, "No," and kept walking.

The younger of the two stepped in front of me, blocking my way and forcing me to stop. The older fellow leaned in and growled, "I know you have a dollar!"

199

I looked around. Other people were certainly within shouting distance. We were alone in our conversation, but this was not a deserted alleyway. The men were emitting a determination laced with violence.

"Come on, give me a dollar!" the older man demanded again.

The younger guy followed up, with a tone of incredulousness, "You don't have a dollar for a couple of vets?"

Maybe they were down on their luck veterinarians. In my assessment, these were not people who had ever served in the military. There is a certain bearing these two lacked, and the fact that they did not recognize me as possessing that bearing was further evidence that they were not actual veterans.

"Oh, you're vets, huh?" I said swelling with anger. I was no longer concerned; I was on solid ground. "Tell me a bit about that. Who did you serve with?"

We went round and round while I established that – while it is possible that they had seen an episode or two of *M*A*S*H* – they had never served in the Armed Forces.

It was all very quick – certainly less than two minutes from their first word to the time I walked away with all of my cash plus two dollars from them – but it was one of my more satisfying experiences at Harvard.

*

The day before I was scheduled to leave Harvard, a woman who identified herself as a Harvard undergrad reached out to me via e-mail. And just like that, my epic record was broken.

She did not exactly offer to bring me into the fold. She was a well-wisher, and she wrote, "I hope your time at Harvard was not too displeasing."

It wasn't displeasing. It wasn't what I had hoped for, but it wasn't a bad experience.

People have asked me why I think the students did not reach out to me. Many of the speculations involve Ivy League stereotypes. Maybe the students were too busy studying? Maybe they were too busy partying? Maybe they saw themselves as above it all and apathetic to the concerns of mere mortals?

My guess was that the undergraduates were somewhere between 18 and 22 years old, away from home, and having a once-in-a-lifetime experience. They were busy and distracted, and appropriately so. I wished things had turned out differently for me there, but I had not an ounce of bitterness towards the students – individually or collectively. They were doing exactly what they should have been doing.

So why did I meet students on other campuses but not at Harvard? Was there a difference between the students at the other schools and the students at Harvard?

I don't think so. The difference was with me, and it was a simple difference. At the other schools, I was luckier. For whatever reason, for 30 days, I lacked the single most important attribute a person can have: Good fortune.

I drove away from Cambridge content. I spent a month prowling like a ghost through the hallowed grounds of Harvard. And like a ghost, I imagine, I missed the feeling of human contact and interaction. I had an opportunity to observe if not to participate. It was not a segment of great passion or high adventure, but it was a learning experience.

I steered my car towards New Jersey without lamenting friends left behind, and I prepared for my final chapter.

PRINCETON UNIVERSITY

Q: How many Princeton students does it take to screw in a light bulb?

A: Two – one to mix the martinis and one to call the electrician.

I have a confession to make: Color matters.

Most schools have official colors in shades of blue or red. Cornell is red, Harvard is red, Brown is red (a funny phrase), Yale is blue, Columbia is blue, Penn is blue *and* red. Perhaps it is my love of variety and bright colors that contributed towards my infatuation of Dartmouth with its green.

Princeton's school colors are orange and black. The black is flattering and the orange is obnoxious, and I love it.

Princeton University – located in a quiet, wealthy, and tree-laden part of New Jersey – sits in the upper echelon of the Ivies alongside Harvard and Yale. But Princeton also sits in the heart of American history.

The university was founded in 1746 and called the College of New Jersey. It moved to Princeton, New Jersey in 1756 – but it did not adopt the name "Princeton" until 1896. The university saw every major event of the United States, from the birth of the nation to the present time.

My favorite story is from the Battle of Princeton during the Revolutionary War. British troops took refuge in Nassau Hall – the first (and, at the time, the only) building of the current campus – inspiring the Americans to fire a cannon at the structure in an effort to drive the Brits out.

It worked. The British forces fled, leaving behind a cannon of their own. The cannon was ultimately buried on campus near Nassau Hall in an area appropriately named the Cannon Green.

Today, the Cannon Green is the site of a winter bonfire that is lit when Princeton's football team beats both Harvard and Yale. At the time of my visit, the Green had not seen a bonfire in more than a decade, but it is that kind of optimism and tradition that inspired me at Princeton.

*

I was off to a great start at Princeton.

I arrived with a pocketful of names – people I had met fortuitously or who had been recommended to me. After my time at Harvard, I was determined to get the scoop from students.

The Daily Princetonian published an article about my expedition. Not only did the article *not* include any depressing reminders about Penn, but it *did* include contact information for me. In one day, I received scores of invitations, including offers from students with places for me to stay.

I had continued my habit of writing to the administration of the schools before I arrived. The folks at Princeton were a delight. They warmed to my project and offered any help they could lend. It made my life easier to know that I was at least not unwelcome.

My first night in town, I knew the stars were aligning in my favor.

I parked my car on Nassau Street around 9 p.m., and walked towards the part of the campus with which I was most familiar. I turned on Washington Road, passing the large structure of Firestone Library on my right. I ambled by Burr Hall – named after alumnus Aaron Burr – and Green Hall – not named after me.

As the Woodrow Wilson School of Public and International Affairs appeared on my left, I considered another sign of my good fortune: The weather. It had been a long winter, but spring was in full swing and summer was right around the corner. It was chilly that evening, and it had rained recently, but the air smelled fresh. It was the scent of the end of the school year. It stirred memories of years – all the way back to elementary school – where I was excited to leave my teachers behind and start thinking about exploring the woods, playing kickball with Shawn Hogan, and going with my family for a week at the beach. I breathed deeply and smiled.

I crossed Washington Road and entered 1879 Hall. The building is the home of the philosophy department. My undergraduate thesis had required that I find an outside examiner, and I was impertinent enough to invite preeminent Princeton philosopher, Margaret Wilson, to serve in this role. She graciously agreed. She became a mentor to me. My goal was to join her at Princeton and continue to study philosophy, but she passed away before I could begin my formal studies with her. Nevertheless, I spent time in the department as an undergraduate student with her and as a graduate student without her, and it has always felt like a safe space to visit.

I left 1879 and began winding my way across campus. The architecture at Princeton always shocks me a bit. Most of the buildings are worth the time to stop and admire individually, but, collectively, they strike me as crazily mismatched.

I passed McCosh Hall, a large L-shaped building with grayish-white limestone walls draped with ivy. It is designed in a gothic style with the bay windows, flying buttresses, and design flourishes that I had come to love in my travels.

The School of Architecture building faces the long part of McCosh's L, and it is a starkly different design. To my untrained eye, the outside of the building looks like the 1970s threw up all over it. It is brick with limestone accents around narrow windows. Where McCosh invites exploration, the Architecture Building can be consumed by the eye at a glance.

I walked behind Nassau Hall. The building had been gutted by fire twice and rebuilt, but its cornerstone dates to 1754. It is a colonial-style building with thick stone walls and a bell tower atop the structure.

Facing the back of Nassau are the buildings of Clio and Whig. These two edifices are not identical twins, but they were definitely sold as a set. They are constructed of white marble with pillars and large, forbidding doors. From the front, they look very much like the temples and crypts occupied by secret societies at other institutions. They are a shocking departure from an already-eclectic collection of architectural styles on campus.

The buildings were commissioned together in the late 1800s to house debates – a Princeton tradition dating back to 1760. The buildings represented two distinct societies that ultimately merged into the American Whig-Cliosophic Society. The group occupied only Whig Hall after the 1920s; Cliosophic Hall eventually served as the office of the Graduate School and as a lobby for the undergraduate admissions office.

As I continued to walk across the campus, I began to hear music on the soft breeze. I looked towards Alexander Hall, knowing that it housed the orchestra. The building is beautiful with two turrets flanking a wall of white rock with horizontal lines of red granite, decorated by a round, four-part stained glass window – a spectacular sight to see. But no sounds emanated from the dark building.

I approached the collegiate gothic structure of Mathey College – one of the residential colleges at Princeton – and immediately recognized the source of the music.

Princeton's campus is as famous for its arches as much as Cornell's is famous for its gorges. The arches are beautiful, architecturally significant, and acoustically interesting. The largest of those arches is the Blair Arch, situated in Mathey College. And it is in this arch that a cappella groups perform.

I stood outside the arch alongside dozens of students listening to the concert. I joined them in loud applause after each number. I reminded myself to hold on to that fleeting moment, and I hoped that the people around me were thinking the same thing.

*

I recognize the importance of timing and the impact that it had on my project. In an academic year, some periods were rife with events, and some were more of a grind. Generally, October offers more tradition and festivities than, say, February at northeastern universities.

I was at Princeton at a good time with commencement around the corner, but I was also able to observe another tradition: Newman's Day.

On April 24th – that is, on 4/24 – some Princeton undergrads set out to drink 24 beers in 24 hours. The day is named after the actor Paul Newman, but the quote that led to the naming of the day is apocryphal. Paul Newman was erroneously credited as saying in a campus talk: "24 hours in a day; 24 beers in a case. Coincidence? I think not."

The year prior to my visit, Paul Newman spoke out loudly against the tradition. The unofficial celebration was observed at Princeton and several other institutions, and Newman's attorney wrote asking to have his name disassociated with the day. It was especially offensive to Newman because he had lost a son to substance abuse, and he did not want to be viewed as contributing to this culture.

The event, however, was in the hands of the students, not the university, and it would take more than an angry letter to come between an undergraduate and his beer.

In the end, the day was not much of a spectacle. A student coming out of Marx Hall yelled, "Happy Newman's Day!" to me. I watched some drunken students play horseshoes – until one of the drunker students grew angry that I was watching. I saw plenty of older community members strolling around, presumably seeking the same debauchery that I hoped to find. Near Blair Arch, I found an inebriated student in his underwear and a young woman with beer breath and a skirt of immodest length.

In other words, I observed just a typical Sunday in the Ivy League.

*

Successful admission to a highly selective school usually requires that applicants are well-rounded, with a breadth of experiences.

I have known people to deliberately attempt to manufacture this breadth. In their senior years of high school, they join the model United Nations or they begin to volunteer at a soup kitchen or they renew their interest in scouting and go to work on their Gold Awards. That is not to say that it is always calculated – or that any calculation that leads to an enriching experience is a bad thing – but successful prospective students understand the value of such pursuits.

Another aspect of character and development that is often on the minds of hopeful students is athletics. A couch potato of a high school sophomore may suddenly work vigorously to earn varsity letters before he applies to college. No doubt more often, athletic students who had always participated in sports continue to participate. In either case, potential students often engage in activities that improve stamina and coordination alongside their studies.

These activities carry over to college life. They are never completely absent, but they become more visible the nicer the weather turns.

Princeton in the late spring is a great place for people who enjoy outdoor activities. Like most universities, Princeton has incredible facilities for exercise and recreation, but two local features make the school especially appealing to me.

The first is Lake Carnegie. The lake sits at the south side of the campus – a long walk down Washington Road. The lake is a tranquil place for a picnic or to take a kayak. It is also stocked with fish, and I saw people – including Princeton students – casting away hoping for a big catch. I was not sure what their intentions were if they caught a fish, but I read signs about campaigns to counteract pollution in the lake that would make me think twice about biting into something that came out of it.

Of course, the lake comes with a dose of history that I find compelling. Princeton's crew team used to have to travel to practice and compete in their sport. An alumnus of the team approached the philanthropist Andrew Carnegie in 1902. Carnegie had an interest in the creation of man-made bodies of water, and he eventually agreed to finance a lake. Working with the university, he began to purchase land around the Millstone River. Once he had acquired the land, the river was dammed and the lake was created. Carnegie donated the acquired land and lake to Princeton in 1906.

The legend is that President Woodrow Wilson – at this point, president of Princeton; subsequently, president of the United States – asked Carnegie for another donation the following year. Carnegie declined, saying, "I have already given you a lake," to which Wilson allegedly replied, "We needed bread and you gave us cake."

My other favorite outdoor site is Princeton Battlefield. Setting out from campus on a nice day, I would jog up Nassau Street and turn on Mercer Street. First, the campus of the Princeton Theological Seminary would appear on my left. Next, I would run past the simple white house once occupied by Albert Einstein. Another mile or so down Mercer and I would arrive at the open green of the battlefield.

The absence of the Mercer Oak was shocking. This colossal 300-year old oak tree stood close to the road – the only growth of its stature in the foreground. It was named after Brigadier General Hugh Mercer of the Continental Army. General Mercer was stabbed by an enemy bayonet in the battle fought on that ground during the Revolutionary War. He rested against the trunk of the tree after refusing to leave his soldiers behind.

I, too, rested under this tree. Its presence gave me peace and instilled in me a sense of perspective.

Alas, the tree died in the time between my experiences at Princeton. On March 3, 2000, a windstorm took down the large branches, and the township took down the trunk afterwards. They planted a sapling – grown from an acorn of the Mercer Oak – in the stump of the grand tree. It was an appropriate gesture, but it did little towards filling me with peace and perspective.

I would turn off the road and head to the left across the battlefield and towards the woods in the background. In those woods were paths and shade and quiet – all of the features I look for in a run or walk.

I spent hours in those woods, thinking about my journey – where I had started and where I still had left to go.

*

Students at other Ivies had plenty of thoughts about Princeton. An undergrad at Cornell once told me that the people at Princeton were so stuffy and straight-laced that the students who wore jeans on campus were considered alternative. At Columbia, I was part of a discussion where the students insisted that the men at Princeton were all short – a claim also made by Skippy and others at MIT. Several undergrads at the other Ivies told tales of visiting Princeton and immediately finding it intolerable.

I don't know what they were talking about.

I witnessed a variety of dress and fashion at the schools, with Brown being an outlier towards the daytime wearing of hemp pajamas, and Penn being at the opposite end of the spectrum with Prada running shoes and Coach grocery bags. I did not recognize a substantial difference between most of the other schools, including Princeton. Princeton students wore their share of jeans.

Similarly, I saw young men of various statures. I had occasion to meet with some members of the men's basketball team, which may have skewed my observations a bit, but I made another observation that may be related. At Princeton, I was struck by how tall some of the women were. Perhaps it dated back to the two young ladies Shawn and I met at Penn, but I noted many women of unusual height. I supposed someone might see a group of Princeton men and women and leap to the assumption that the men were short rather than that the women were tall.

And whatever pheromones in the air scared off my friends from the other schools, they had no impact on me.

That is not to say that Princeton did not have its unusual quirks. I discovered several of them while meeting with Angela – an attractive and upbeat freshman from California.

Angela had invited me to see her room in Rockefeller – or Rocky – College. Rocky was paired with Mathey, and they looked very similar: Gothic structures of dark stone on the outside, bright and richly appointed common rooms on the inside. Angela's room had a large window overlooking the courtyard below.

We talked about the housing system at Princeton. The colleges are similar in structure and amenities as the colleges at Yale, but they are deployed quite differently. The freshmen and sophomores are assigned to one of five residential colleges, and they live there immediately upon arrival to campus. In junior and senior year, however, students often move out to live in on-campus, apartment-style housing. The residential colleges lack the pull and social significance of their counterparts at some other Ivies.

Angela generously agreed to show me the other residential colleges. We crossed University Place and trekked to Forbes College. The college was built on the site of an inn overlooking the Princeton golf course, and it was as warm and inviting as any inn. We wound our way around construction that would soon become the sixth residential college: Whitman College, financed by and named for business tycoon and alumna, Meg Whitman. Angela guided me to the pair of Wilson College and Butler College. We toured dining halls and common areas, and she connected with friends and classmates at every stop.

As we walked through these residences, Angela mentioned in passing that she was a member of a sorority.

"Wouldn't you want to live in the sorority house?" I inquired.

"Oh, we don't have a house," she replied. "We're not even recognized by the university."

"What does it mean to not be recognized?"

She thought for a couple of seconds and replied, "It means that we're about a heartbeat away from being disallowed."

She was right. Where some Ivies were enmeshed with Greek life, Princeton engaged in a contentious relationship. The previous summer, the administration sent a letter to incoming freshmen discouraging them from participating in the Greek system. It did not have a major impact on pledging, but it signaled clear aggression towards the fraternities and sororities.

The result was a Greek system with not much for me to explore.

Angela and I ended up sitting outside of The Bent Spoon eating homemade ice cream and talking about what I should explore instead: *The Eating Clubs*.

This was another peculiarity of Princeton that students across my journey had mentioned. They were usually discussed in such derisive tones that I actually thought of the words in Italics. Somehow, the phrase bespoke of elitism and oddity.

I thanked Angela for her time, company, and ice cream and set off to learn more about eating clubs.

It turns out that the eating clubs are, in part, a path around earlier prohibitions on fraternities and secret societies. They are similar to both – non-university owned social houses. The clubs were located in mansions of varying character and charm along Prospect Avenue, referred to as "the Street." The houses had common rooms, libraries, computer labs, and other amenities for socializing and passing time. Thursday and Saturday nights, the Street came alive with house parties, dances, and live music. On this last point, the clubs were able to attract high-caliber acts, including Ben Folds, around the time of my visit. The clear majority of upperclassmen at Princeton join these clubs, paying approximately the same price they would have paid the university for a meal plan, and eating their meals with their comrades in the clubs.

The eating clubs fall into two categories.

The first are "sign-in" clubs. The five houses at the time of my visit – Colonial Club, Campus Club, Terrace Club, Quadrangle Club, and Cloister Inn – were billed as non-selective. A student who wants to join simply signs up in the second term of sophomore year. If more people sign up than the club could accommodate, the club would conduct a lottery to select members. Those not selected would ultimately end up in one of the other clubs, I was assured. If you want an eating club, you will get one.

The second type of eating club is the "bicker" clubs. Six organizations fell under this category at the time: The Ivy Club, University Cottage Club, Cap and Gown Club, Princeton Tower Club, Princeton Charter Club, and Tiger Inn. These clubs were decidedly selective. Students engaged in the bicker process by attending the houses they wanted to join upon returning from intersession break in their sophomore years. In the case of some houses, they were subjected to interviews; in the case of others, they engaged in less tame activities as a part of the bicker process. It is hard for a lay person such as me to describe without relying on Greek terms such as "rush" or "pledge."

I experienced several clubs, with mixed results. My first trip as a guest to a sign-in club was unimpressive. The food was not especially appealing, but it was also almost gone when I arrived – perhaps because of the time of day of my visit. I watched my host take the last piece of bread, so I enjoyed a pita sandwich minus the pita. The outside of the mansion was striking, but inside was a mostly unadorned room with lots of simple round tables. My host and I chatted happily for an hour, but no other students said hello to him or talked to us. It left me feeling like the social club was not especially social.

I also took meals in some of the swanky and exclusive eateries of the Street. In these bicker clubs, the atmosphere was much more congenial. The students I met seemed integrated into the social network of their clubs. The food was more plentiful and decent than my first experience, but the clubs were reminiscent of the many fraternity and sorority houses I had experienced in my travels. They were beautiful on the outside, but often damaged, worn, or strangely decorated on the inside.

As the weather got nicer, I saw more of the outdoor social life of the eating clubs. I joined students at a variety of cook-outs and parties on the Street. By the end of

House Party Weekend, I was *almost* a fan of the eating clubs.

I still harbored some hesitation when it came to endorsing the eating clubs. Some of it was due to my own preferences and peccadillos, I'm sure, but some of it came from my conversations with other undergraduates.

For example, I had a conversation with two upperclassmen in their 1903 Hall dorm room. Stephan was refreshed from a visit home to Northern Africa over spring break; Jagdeep was a Sikh student from Kansas. Both students expressed their love of Princeton. Although they came from very different cultures, they had concerns coming into this new environment in a post-9/11 world, but both reported an accepting if inquisitive atmosphere at the university. They were active members of the community, spreading a message of tolerance. They told me they would choose Princeton again given a choice. The only sign of doubt came from Stephan, who admitted that he would have picked Harvard if Harvard would have picked him – but only because, according to him, Harvard Medical School accepts 40% of its own undergrads. Everybody was happy, nothing to complain about.

Our conversation was nearing dinner time, and I inquired casually about eating clubs. Frankly, I was hungry and thought we might grab something to eat together. When I inquired to which eating clubs they belonged, I was not expecting drama. But as soon as I asked, their demeanors changed drastically.

"We have nothing to do with those groups," said Stephan testily.

Jagdeep elaborated, "We are two of about 70 seniors who are independent. That is, not in an eating club."

"Why did you make that choice?" I wondered.

They looked at each other. "They're cliquey," Jagdeep said. "They perpetuate a culture of exclusivity."

"Yeah," agreed Stephan. "They're stupid."

When the ambassadors of tolerance were so adamant, I figured I might want to reserve judgment and let people decide for themselves.

*

Throughout my project, I had to balance my love of classroom learning. I had an ambitious task in front of me; I could not accomplish all of my goals while indulging in lectures, labs, and seminars. But I yearned to explore every subject.

Princeton held special appeal for me on this front. The university has a history of famous and engaging professors.

The example that springs to mind is also one that is not quite accurate: Albert Einstein. He was associated in my mind – and perhaps in the common lexicon – with Princeton University. In fact, he was never a professor at Princeton.

Einstein visited Princeton in 1921 – the same year in which he received the Nobel Prize in Physics – to deliver five lectures on his theory of relativity. In return, he received an honorary doctorate from Princeton.

He returned to the area more than a decade later and assumed a post in the Institute for Advanced Study. The Institute is situated close to Princeton University, and Einstein lived and socialized in the borough of Princeton, but he was not a professor at Princeton.

Nevertheless, I was determined to explore physics during my short stay. I spent time in Jadwin Hall – a science building nestled between Washington Road and Princeton Stadium – slipping into classes and labs. On some occasions, I was accompanied by my new friend Jagdeep who was a physics major.

I discovered a fascinating world in this subculture at Princeton. The physics students were intensely smart and dedicated. They worked with astoundingly expensive equipment in some cases – with Slinkys or rolls of toilet paper in others – on complex mathematical problems. They produced research independently and jointly with faculty. They attempted to explain the big and small of the universe, and it was a pleasure to listen to them explain their work.

I also discovered that I had made some shrewd choices in my life. I may be well suited for philosophy or law, but I am ill-equipped to handle the specificity and rigor of advanced mathematics.

A glutton for punishment, I decided that I needed to spend time in the Department of Mathematics at Princeton. In this case, it had less to do with learning about math and more about witnessing the rare marriage of pop culture and elite academics.

My project followed on the heels of the book, *A Beautiful Mind,* by Sylvia Nassar and the movie of the same name. These works tell the heartbreaking, albeit dramatized, tale of John Nash – a Princeton-educated mathematician who suffered from acute paranoid schizophrenia, and who later in life was awarded the Nobel Prize for his work in game theory. The movie depicts an aging Nash in a Princeton library, scrawling mathematical formulae on windows and blackboards.

The bit that I find most intriguing is that, for all of the storytelling and editing that must go into a tale to make it consumable in a movie-sized bite, the late-night equation scribbling seemed to mirror real life. Nash was commonly referred to as the "Phantom of Fine Hall" and was known for his haunting of the math department, writing out equations in public spaces at all hours.

Professor Nash may have been present during my time on campus, but our paths did not cross. I did, however, sit in on a couple of lower-level math courses that kept me awake, but otherwise did little to prepare me to better appreciate the work of my physicist friends.

I wanted to follow the advice of students on which courses to sample, and they were not short on suggestions. Most of the options I received – I'm sure as a factor of the crowd with which I found myself – were in the hard sciences. I longed for a taste of the humanities.

I found what I needed when I met Lizzie. We met organically when I accidentally stepped on her foot while standing in line at Hoagie Haven – a Princeton must-visit restaurant. As I apologized, she responded amiably that she was a dancer and quite accustomed to people stepping on her toes. I bought her a hoagie and we talked about all things Princeton.

When she told me that she was finishing her junior year, I asked her about the eating clubs. She bickered at the Ivy Club, she told me with a smile, but she was not picked, so she chose an "okay" sign-in club. She lived in Butler College – which she described as the "worst residential college" – in her freshman year, and she was glad to be living in Dod Hall this year. She was older than the typical junior, having taken time away after her freshman year to volunteer for a nonprofit working in Central Africa. Her role there, in part, was to teach impoverished children to dance.

All the while she talked, her smile never left her face. She was pretty – a young, athletic woman with shining brown hair and sparkling blue eyes – but her attitude made her charm irresistible. I loved her optimism and happiness.

For a week, we met every day. She told me tales of Africa and Arkansas, and I told her stories from the Ivy League. She walked me through Alexander Hall, and I walked her through the trails of Princeton Battlefield. She offered to teach me some basic dance steps, and I offered to teach her to sing Irish folk songs – but we were each too scared. We talked and laughed, two unusual characters crossing paths in unlikely circumstances.

She invited me to attend her Introduction to Music course. We sat together in the heights of a sloping auditorium in McCosh Hall. The huge windows to the right revealed the green leaves of mature trees; the windows to the left provided a view of the Chapel – one of my favorite buildings on campus. We sat in black, plastic chairs and listened to a renowned music professor educate us on the minimalists and maximalists of the post-modern era.

The last class of the term was nearing an end, and Lizzie and I could feel a shift in the energy of the room. The sleepers in the class awoke, students seemed to sit just a bit taller, and I leaned in to gather the last bits of wisdom offered by the prof.

The music professor paused for effect, and then said perhaps the most meaningful statement I heard in my year of travels:

"Life. What is it but a...?"

Perhaps it was meaningful, or perhaps it wasn't. Both Lizzie and I missed the last word. We looked at each other with equal measures of confusion, and shrugged. It didn't sound like "dream," and we couldn't come up with a viable alternative. The meaning of life, perhaps, slipped through our fingers!

The professor continued on to say, "That is the end of the course. Thank you."

The room erupted in applause, which the professor returned to his pupils.

"So that's it for your classes?" I asked Lizzie, amidst the chaos of students gathering their belongings and leaving the room. "What's next?"

"I have a couple of papers due that I really have to get on before Dean's Date Rush."

We agreed that we would connect again the next week to observe another Princeton tradition. At 5 p.m. on the last Tuesday of the term, all written work is due. Students show up in the McCosh Courtyard for a party with music and food to cheer on the undergraduates who procrastinated on their papers. The 5 p.m. deadline was taken very seriously, as was procrastination. As a result, it was not uncommon to see sweat-stained students running into McCosh Hall at 4:58.

It was a great celebration. The students partying did not disappoint, nor did the scholars jogging in to turn in their work. It was a good event to witness as a part of my research, but it was marred by one detail: Lizzie never showed up.

I like to believe she was too busy dancing, with her telltale smile firmly in place, to make it.

*

As the end of the term approached, my new friends began to ask me if I intended to stay for reunion weekend. I began by demurring – stating that my project was about current students, not alumni – but my new friends were convincing. It is a key ritual, they said, and current undergrads participate in the event. It is a great opportunity for them to network, and the alumni love to see the undergraduates.

The weekend before commencement, the campus is flooded by more than 20,000 Princeton alumni. At most universities, I would expect to see classes gathering in five- and 10-year increments – for example, the classes of 2000, 1995, 1990, 1985, etc. – but Princeton reunions have representatives of all classes in between. With the underclassmen absent from campus, the returning alumni were permitted to stay in on-campus housing. I can only imagine the nostalgic treat it was for someone 10 or 20 or 50 years out of Princeton to return to living on campus. And, knowing the relative discomfort of grown-ups living in communal and cramped space, I can only imagine the joy that must accompany returning to real life at the end of the weekend.

The pivotal event of alumni weekend occurred on Saturday: The P-rade. This was where tradition, costume design, and enthusiasm met.

The affair began on Nassau Street – an ample road for most occasions, but it was tested as a staging area for all of the revelers. I surveyed the scene with Stephan and Jagdeep before entering the campus. As seniors, they had a defined role to play, but they sat with me by Dillon Gym for the first bit of the parade.

The noise of the approaching P-rade was deafening. The first in the line-up was the Princeton University Band. They seemed much more organized and cohesive – but more stoic and less fun – than the CUMB.

After the band, the alumni fell into a decisive pecking order – the oldest people and classes first, followed in succession by younger and younger classes. The older classes marched past the younger ones, who cheered for their older peers before falling in line behind them.

But the group that fell in immediately behind the band was the class celebrating their 25th year reunion. The 25th reunion class always follow the band. Alumni of the graduate school marched in the line-up where that class should have been.

Once the band passed and the 25th year reunion class passed, I observed a golf cart leading several others. The single oldest alumnus participated in a place of honor. In this case, the person with seniority was a gentleman from the class of 1925. He was at least 100 years old, I imagine, and smiling from his seat on the golf cart. He held a silver cane presented to him by the university president as a sign of his station.

As the masses came on, I recognized the oddity of their dress. Stephan explained the unusual attire of some of the alumni. The more significant the year of the reunion and the more alumni were attending, the more elaborately they planned their theme. I saw plenty of orange and

221

black, but the dress code was not restrictive. I saw what I believe was a Hawaiian theme, and I saw a group that may have been a gaggle of over educated Elvi – which, as you probably know, is the plural of "Elvis."

My undergrad friends educated me on the topic of the locomotive cheer. As classes went by, the crowd of alumni, families, current students, and other community members would hiss and hoot and holler, shouting "Hip, hip, hip! Rah, rah, rah! Tiger, tiger, tiger! Sis, sis, sis! Boom, boom, boom! Ahhh..." followed by the class year. The marching classes would return the calls to the crowds.

Adding to the cacophony and mayhem were a variety of entertainers: Horse-drawn carriages, jugglers, and all sorts of musical acts, ranging from high school marching bands to barber shop quartets. Stephan informed me that reunion classes sometimes paid performers to precede them in the parade. This was the first reunion weekend that Stephan and Jagdeep attended, but they did not seem at all shocked by the sorts of acts we witnessed.

As we watched and cheered, I would occasionally see a face in the crowd that looked familiar. I had met so many people in the preceding months that everyone began to look familiar. *Is that Heather from Cornell? That guy looks like the Greek Mythology professor from Penn!* And, of course, I kept catching imagined glimpses of people from Princeton. *Did I just see Lizzie? Is that Lizzie under that tree? Lizzie?* No, on all counts.

The classes were filing by and I was suppressing my urge to call out to familiar-looking strangers, when I saw another familiar face. The chances of me knowing someone who was back for his 50th year Princeton reunion was negligible. Nevertheless, I could not shake the feeling that I knew a man who was proudly striding in the parade, waving to the crowd.

Finally, I turned to Jagdeep and yelled over the noise, "I know that guy."

He smiled patiently and replied, "Of course you do." When I still could not come up with a name, he said, "That's Ralph Nader, the politician."

Here he was, several hundred miles, six months, and many schools later. The presidential race over and his talk at Brown long behind him, he was just one of the tens of thousands of alumni who had descended on the campus.

In a year of leaving people behind, I felt like I was seeing an old friend. I cheered loudly and put some extra oomph in my locomotive for the class of 1955.

Jagdeep and Stephan begged off to go and join the senior class. They were staging to rush Poe Field – the end of the parade route – to be officially welcomed by the president as alumni.

I walked against the flow of the P-rade and looked at the FitzRandolph Gate. Just like many schools with a gate – most notably Brown University – the lore of the institution warned against passing through at the wrong time. Those who pass through those gates prior to commencement were doomed to never graduate.

It seemed late in the season, and I was not even a Princeton student, but I respectfully exited through a side gate and made my way to The Bent Spoon. My energy was flagging, and I hoped a scoop of Coconut Streak would be just what I needed.

*

The last day of May was a warm sunny day. The skies were a majestic, cloudless blue; the tall trees covered with green leaves seemed ripe with history and tradition.

The graduating seniors at Princeton were 1,123 strong, accompanied by almost 700 graduate students earning master's degrees or doctorates. With guests, the area in front of Nassau Hall was flooded by more than 8,000 people facing the oldest campus building, its brown stone walls covered with climbing ivy. A large white banner with the orange and black school seal served as a backdrop to the stage filled with distinguished academics, officers of the institution – including then-President Shirley Tilghman – members of the Board of Trustees, and the most honored guests.

On Sunday, two days earlier and at the tail end of reunion weekend, the university held its Baccalaureate ceremony in the chapel. The chapel seemed huge until a thousand or so people were stuffed inside.

I watched with other well-wishers on a simulcast set up in the quad formed by the chapel, Dickinson Hall and McCosh Hall. We watched the seniors filing in to the chapel, led by a bagpiper that grabbed both the joy and sorrow of reaching an academic milestone. We sat on uncomfortable chairs drinking bottles of water and listening to the talk delivered by a Princeton professor who earned the Pulitzer Prize, the American Book Award, and the Nobel Prize: Toni Morrison. She was only days away from receiving an honorary doctorate in recognition of her work from Oxford University – one of a handful of schools that I might place in a class above the Ivies in the U.S.

The next day, I joined the seniors for the tradition of Class Day, a day that was described in 1898 – more than *40 years after* its inception – as "a day over which the Graduating Class has full charge and which we run to suit ourselves, in our characteristic way."

One of those characteristic ways was the donning of senior class jackets, or beer jackets. The name comes from the class of 1912 that recognized the wisdom of wearing an outer garment to avoid the beer stains they otherwise might incur on this day. Each class creates a unique design – typically involving the colors and symbols of Princeton. The jackets of the seniors on this occasion were black with orange cuffs, and a dynamic-looking orange tiger and graduation year emblazoned on the back.

The class gathered behind Nassau Hall on the Cannon Green on this warm and sunny Monday morning. Speeches were made, awards and prizes were bestowed on selected students, and the keynote speaker took the stage. The students were pursuing a comedy theme in recent selections. In the two preceding years, the speakers were Jon Stewart and Jerry Seinfeld; the current speaker was Chevy Chase.

All of the celebrations at the end of four years of work (for the undergrads; one year for me) had led to this day. A Tuesday like so many others. But on this particular day, we were reveling and moving to a new chapter in our lives.

The ceremony had the pomp and circumstance one would expect from such an occasion. It was rich in moments.

One such moment was the conferring of honorary degrees. Perhaps that act is so striking to me because of the value I place on a college degree. The degree is the culmination of an incredible amount of work; it symbolizes attained knowledge and recognizes a high level of accomplishment. To have an institution bestow such an honor in recognition of achievement is a laudation of exceptional value.

The other related reason why I was so mesmerized by the conferring of these honors was because of the high-caliber recipients. I sat and watched as people such as the founder of a major mutual fund group, the chief executive of the Philadelphia Museum of Art, a Nobel Laureate and poet, an emeritus professor of Romance languages and literature, and an astronomer received their awards. I was suitably impressed by each of them reading their biographies, but the sixth awardee needed no biography or introduction to impress the crowd: The cellist Yo-Yo Ma.

225

Another moment worth mentioning was the speech of the Latin Salutatorian. While "salutatorian" typically means the second highest graduate in the class, the term is a bit more subjective at Princeton. The faculty selects the Salutatorian based on academics, but also on language ability – because, in fact, the address of the Salutatorian is traditionally delivered in Latin.

As if this were not cool enough, the graduating seniors have a different program than family members, guests, and spectators. In the program distributed to the graduating class, the speech is transcribed in English. It also includes prompts for laughter, excitement, and other reactions.

Thus, when the Salutatorian stated in Latin, "Few people know that the Romans once captured Princeton, but as a history major I can assure you it's true. Check Tacitus, it's somewhere in the back," the class burst into loud laughter – surprising, perplexing, and impressing the majority of the uninformed spectators.

The moment that I found the most poignant – which should be no surprise, since it is a moment designed to be poignant – was the speech of the Valedictorian, Varun Kishor Phadke.

Varun is the third undergraduate in this book to be identified by his name, and I cite him for the same reasons that I credited two Yalies with their real names.

First, his name is a matter of public record. His title as Valedictorian was widely published, and it would be especially weird to assign a pseudonym to the holder of such an honor.

Second, he deserves all of the honor we can heap on. Valedictorian at Princeton University, heading for Harvard Medical School upon graduation. I met him only once in passing on campus – a modest, soft spoken, and funny young man – and I had to suppress my natural urge to tell him how inspired I was by his achievements. Now that I am temporally and geographically removed, I'll say it: Very well done, Varun!

On this sunny Tuesday, however, it was not his accomplishments or potential that captivated me – it was his speech.

I arrived with freshmen at Cornell in August, and I was sitting with the seniors at Princeton in May. It felt like I had crammed four years of experience into my head in just one academic year. I was tired, but enthusiastic. Much like the graduating class, I was done with the last chapter and eager for the next. Perhaps that is why the speech resonated so much with me.

There were funny parts. He mused about why he was selected as Valedictorian. He pointed out that both he and the then-president of Princeton were molecular biologists. He further noted that the previous two Valedictorians were also molecular biologists. "Now of course, as we all know, correlation does not imply causation," he said. "But as they say in our business, these findings merit further study."

Varun went on to offer "words of wisdom" to his classmates, such as:

"Don't be nervous. Remember, it could always be worse. For example, in my case, *all* the Nobel laureates could be here."

And:

"Appreciate simple things. Like birds. Before my thesis I knew nothing about them. I still don't, but I would like to."

But it was how he ended his speech that touched me most:

"In closing, allow me to perform the duty actually required of the Valedictorian. In fact, being the conscientious, but non-Latin-speaking individual that I am, after Dean Williams broke the news to me, I went home and looked up what 'valedictorian' actually meant. According to my sources, the Valedictorian is the student

227

chosen to bid farewell on behalf of the graduating class. Leaving aside self-deprecation for the time being, I know for a fact that this is something I cannot do. As President Tilghman said yesterday, today we may be graduating, but we will never truly leave Princeton. Therefore, I cannot honestly say farewell. The best I can do is to say: Classmates, teachers, friends: Until we meet again."

Afterwards, caps were thrown, but not as many as I would have predicted.

Photos were taken by family members – thousands more than I could have predicted.

Music was played, cookies were eaten, and hugs were exchanged.

I walked out through the FitzRandolph Gates along with the seniors. I turned and enjoyed one last look at the campus before getting into my car.

Then I drove away from Princeton, awash in a mix of emotion. My year in the Ivy League was over.

EPILOGUE

Q: How many writers does it take to screw in a light bulb?

A: One, but it may take him 10 years to do it.

The graduation ceremony at Princeton was almost a decade ago as I sit here typing this.

I finished my research on schedule. I had plenty of notes and contacts – setting my time at Harvard aside – and I had a chapter written and others well underway. All that was left was to tie it up and release it to the world.

But I didn't. I walked away from the project. Occasionally, I would grab one of my old notebooks and flip through it reminiscing, or I would look back at the travelogue I published online during my journey. A couple of times, I considered writing. I suppose I may have even adjusted a word or two in the manuscripts. But I made no concerted effort to finish the book. My notes grew dusty, and I began responding to inquiries with the news that the book would not be released. Ever.

I returned from my project with a great fatigue and a little sadness. I was coming from a state of near-homelessness, with major changes every 30 days. I made friends and left them in a span of weeks. I had looked upon the rare and the beautiful – and then I walked away from it. There were moments of tension and bouts of boredom. Sometimes I was welcome, sometimes I was not; sometimes I was an insider, sometimes I was invisible. I was tired and bruised, emotionally. I believe I was in something akin to a state of shock.

People asked me about my adventures. My family, Shawn Hogan, Katie, and people I had interacted with along the way. I was inundated by the curious and the eager. I had no energy to tell my stories. It was difficult to straddle the divide between my project and the life that was spread before me upon my return.

Life has a way of moving forward – whether a person is willing or not – and soon the project was behind me. It slipped into a private place in my mind, a place where only I could visit.

But I had plenty of reminders of my year in the Ivy League. I enrolled in graduate programs at other top-tier schools, studying new subjects and pursuing new degrees. Following my passion, I ended up working in higher education. I served as a professor and as a dean, and I continue to work as a university administrator. I even ended up living in the northeast in an area surrounded by Ivy League schools.

*

One fall day, I found myself in New Haven, Connecticut walking across the campus at Yale on my way to a meeting. It was my first time back on the campus since I left during fall final exams a decade earlier.

I looked longingly but briefly at Harkness Tower as I passed it. I remembered a snowy day when I was almost flattened by a bicycle near that spot, and I smiled.

As I passed in front of Sterling Memorial Library, I saw a family that was obviously lost. The mother had four kids in tow, the oldest of which looked to be in the market for college, and the mom was casting about with her eyes seeking some sort of assistance.

I stopped and asked her if I could help.

"We came to visit Yale, but now that we're here, we don't really know where to go."

"Come on," I said with a smile. "I'll take you to the Admissions Office."

As we walked, I began pointing out some of the sights, introducing the family to Old Campus and some of the residential colleges we passed.

The mother volunteered that they had been visiting Columbia that morning. Turning to the daughter, I asked, "You aren't interested in the marching band, are you?"

"No," she responded.

"Good, let me tell you about this one time . . ." I told her a story.

One of her brothers, about 14 years old, questioned me, "Will we go by the Yale School of Forestry?"

I pointed towards Science Hill. "It's over there. Great school. Is forestry something you might be interested in?" When he acknowledged that it was, it led me to a tangent about Dartmouth and how the Appalachian Trail cuts right through the campus.

The mother spoke up again and said hopefully, "Our little road trip will actually take us to Harvard. I don't suppose you know much about them?"

"No, not much," I confessed. "But wait: Are you going to Brown on your way?"

Mother and daughter looked at each other. "It really wasn't on our radar. Why?"

"Well, it isn't for everyone, but it has some great qualities. And some great food. If you decide to go, there is a woman in admissions – probably in her mid-to-late hundreds – that you should say hi to for me . . ."

When we arrived at Yale Admissions, the mother thanked me and wondered aloud, "How do you know so much about all of these schools?" The kids stood still and attentive waiting to see what story I would tell next.

"I once spent 30 days at each of the Ivy League schools, living with students, attending classes, and participating in campus life over the course of an academic year."

"You know," suggested the daughter, helpfully, "you should write a book."

So I did.

*

231

What did I learn from my adventures?

I suppose there are a number of pithy and true answers:

- o I learned bits about mathematics, music, physics, sociology, and political science that continue to plague my thoughts today.
- o I can finally relate and contribute to conversations involving fraternity parties.
- o I can find a good meal in Providence; but I smile widest when I remember eating peanut butter sandwiches in Cambridge.
- o I know to embrace a Zen-like state of acceptance when parking in West Philly, which I still do several times a year.
- o I can make some good choices when I meet a smiling dog, a person with a pointy chin, or a witty and brilliant psychology professor.
- o I learned that a cappella is surprisingly sexy; and that marching band, unsurprisingly, is not.

Most of what I learned, however, was about myself. In a book about one man's journeys, it is hardly surprising that the lessons are more about the man than the journey. I know myself better for having undertaken and completed the exploration. I learned about the capacity and limits of my own optimism, tolerance, preferences, and appetite for adventure.

A big part of my learning was about the kindness of others. So many people, who had no reason to help me, did. They shared their stories and gave their time and answered my questions. Students, professors, and friends kept me safe and informed. People invited me into their lives, homes, and organizations. I am still moved when I think of the help I had, and I will never be able to adequately express my gratitude for those who were a part of this expedition.

I am still a school snob. I still place a premium on educational pedigree. I still wear school gear – a red Cornell sweatshirt as I type this.

But I no longer put the Ivy League on a pedestal. I admire the schools – all of them – but they are no longer as mysterious as they were. I do not pretend that I am an insider or a member of an exclusive family just because of my project, but it has provided me with some perspective on the institutions. I have experienced some version of them. I have seen the good and the bad, and I walk away with my eyes wide open. My love has been replaced by a powerful respect.

These places – Cornell, Brown, Dartmouth, Yale, Penn, Columbia, Harvard, and Princeton – places that most people only hear of, are real. More magical than I can describe, but real. The students who attend these schools are real young adults with complicated lives, remarkable intellects, and incredible potential. I was inspired by the paths they took to get to where they were, the opportunities that they had open in front of them, and the lives they were living when I met them.

And that is what I learned in college: I learned how interesting a life can be that is seized and fully lived.

I can't wait to see what happens tomorrow.

The Things I Learned in College

ACKNOWLEDGEMENTS

I went into this project as a fan of the people of the Ivy League, and I emerge impressed and inspired by the people I met, places I saw, and experiences I collected. It has been a rare privilege to explore these institutions.

First and foremost, I am deeply grateful to the people who helped me along the way. Many of these were students, administrators, and faculty at the Ivies; others were friends who provided their support and advice. Every day was an adventure filled with people who were willing to lend their time and assistance. Most of what I learned was because of them.

Of special concern on my journey was the matter of sleeping. At each school and on every night, I relied on the kindness of others to keep me indoors. This group of friends is responsible for my sanity and safety, and I am certainly thankful for their help.

I am also grateful to my editors and readers who helped to shape this work into its current state. Many people contributed – including Patti Blair, RaeAnne Cordova, and especially Lindsey Ryan – and we all benefit from their improvements.

On the technical side – which is where I suffer my biggest bouts of anxiety-induced procrastination – I am indebted to Katie Coates for her cover design and to Luke Moore for all of his Web assistance. I may have driven them crazy, but they handled it with grace.

And, of course, I must thank Jason, Shawn, and Katie for being in my life and in my book. Their contributions to this work make me laugh. I hope they emerge as the beloved characters they are.

Furthermore, I am sincerely thankful for you, my dear reader. You chose to enter into a relationship with this book, and I do not take that for granted. I hope you enjoyed our time together. Feel free to connect with me on social media and to reach out with questions. And please consider publishing a positive review of the book and recommending it to your literate and curious friends. After all, we are all in this together now.

This project was two years of hard effort separated by a decade of neglect. My life has changed a great deal in a decade, and I have two distinct groups of supporters from these two time periods. The people who made the research possible in their own ways were Lauren Newman and Beth Colvin – two fiercely strong and undeniably lovely people. The writing of this book and the path of my life was deeply impacted by Christine McGrail and all she has given me. In all candor, this book simply would not exist without the encouragement, support, and brains of Stephanie Fowell. If my path had not intersected with the four of you, I don't know where I would be.

Finally, I am grateful for my father, John, and my children – Jack, Zoe, and Will – for all they did and didn't do in support of this project.

About the Author

Sean-Michael Green was a terrible high school student, barely graduating with poor grades. He found college years later, and discovered an aptitude and intellectual curiosity that surprised him. He earned degrees at the University of Pittsburgh, Marist College, the University of Pennsylvania, and Cornell University; and he studied at Columbia, Carnegie Mellon, and the Sorbonne. Today, he works as an administrator at a university.

Prior to pursuing his dream of working in higher education, Sean-Michael served as a United States Marine, an attorney, an entrepreneur, a hotel clerk (for about three hours), an Emergency Medical Technician, and a stand-up comedian.

He lives in the northeast of the United States, surrounded by Ivy League schools.

More information is available at
www.SeanMichaelGreen.com.

www.ingramcontent.com/pod-product-compliance
Lightning Source LLC
Chambersburg PA
CBHW071955040426
42447CB00009B/1350